Slow
Cooker
Cooking

Slow Cooker Cooking

Lora Brody

wm.

WILLIAM MORROW
75 YEARS OF PUBLISHING
An Imprint of HarperCollins*Publishers*

This book is dedicated to David and Jon Strymish—first, for their friendship; and then, for all the years of encouragement and support they have given not only me but every other author lucky enough to stumble across them in the cluttered aisles of the New England Mobile Book Fair. They are booksellers in the finest sense of the tradition, and the reading world is a better place thanks to them.

HarperCollins books may be purchased for educational, business, or sales promotional use. For information please write: Special Markets Department, HarperCollins Publishers Inc., 10 East 53rd Street, New York, NY 10022.

FIRST EDITION

Designed by Lee Fukui

Printed on acid-free paper

Library of Congress Cataloging-in-Publication Data

Brody, Lora, 1945–
Slow cooker cooking / by Lora Brody. — 1st ed.
p. cm.
ISBN 0-688-17471-X
1. Electric cookery, slow. I. Title.
TX827 .B72 2001
641.5'884—dc21   00–058239

00 01 02 03 04 QW 10 9 8 7 6 5 4 3 2 1

Contents

Acknowledgments

"Oh, I'd love to be your recipe tester!" Whenever someone says this to me, I just smile ruefully, shake my head, and don't even bother to try to explain what a tedious, mind-numbing, demanding job it can be. Very few recipes turn out just right the first, second, or even third time. Preparing veal stew four times or eight variations of black bean soup makes you yearn for something sweet—until you have to test Indian pudding again and again. Every once in a while a recipe works on the first try, but more often than not you have to make yet another trip to the supermarket for ingredients that go into dishes your family, the neighbors, and even the fire department are all too eager to turn down because they haven't finished off the last batch of food you sent over.

The reason I am still walking and talking after working on this book is directly related to the extraordinary patience, dogged determination, quasi-obsessive attention to detail, and unfailing good humor of my friend and colleague Emmy Clausing, who not only tests (and retests) my recipes but also develops her own fair share of them. Then she sharpens her pencil (as it were) and edits the text, making sure that when a recipe calls for butter, it's two tablespoons, not twenty. Emmy is the original "can do" person, and I am blessed to be in the company of such a wealth of positive and affirming energy. I am grateful, as well, to Laura Ford, Rose Mary Schaefer, and Reggie Dwork, whose creative input, enthusiasm, and recipe-testing skills made this a better book. I would especially like to thank my wonderful agent, Susan Ginsburg, who promised me that this book would see the light of day. I believe I owe her a trip to Paris.

Introduction

I've been a slow cooker addict ever since I received one as a wedding present almost thirty-five years ago. Back then we *all* used slow cookers. With the help of a slow cooker, a young bride could turn an inexpensive cut of meat into a tender stew, stretching the grocery budget in the process. We used this appliance to make chili, beans, and dozens of different soups and stews. When asked, "How did you have the time to cook this?" we answered apologetically, "Oh, I did it in the slow cooker," as if this were a trifle embarrassing.

There was a certain reluctance to admit that you had made dinner using such a homely, unsophisticated appliance. It was a little like admitting you'd used an eggbeater instead of a wire whisk to beat egg whites for a soufflé.

As cooking became more of a leisure activity and sexier equipment, such as gleaming copper pots, turbo food processors, and espresso/capuccino machines, became kitchen essentials in many homes, the slow cooker was shoved farther back in the closet, stored in the basement, or sold off at yard sales.

Yet sales have continued. The appliance obviously fills an important need. I never put away or gave away my slow cooker. When I was writing *Plugged In*, I hauled it out to create and test recipes. I also went out and bought several dozen new slow cookers and was delighted to see that manufacturers had listened to consumers and now made attractive models in many sizes and in solid primary colors. I collected dozens of "traditional" recipes from magazines and newspapers for dishes that I suspected could, with some adjustments, be made in the slow cooker. Every time I saw the word "bistro" or "braised" or came across something that needed more than an hour's cooking time or required continuous stirring over low heat, I grabbed my scissors and clipped the recipe.

My hunch paid off. When the *New York Times* ran a recipe for cassoulet that required dozens of steps and hours of careful pot watching, I was able to convert it into a recipe that had a third fewer steps and cooked beautifully in an unwatched pot. The more I used the slow cooker to make nontraditional, sophisticated dishes, the more I realized its potential.

If you are a loyal slow cooker user, none of the things I'm about to say will come as a surprise. You already know how succulent, moist, and flavorful foods become when they are cooked slowly and gently in the appliance's closed environment. You understand that the toughest cuts of meat can be cooked until they are tender enough to be cut with a fork.

You already know all this, and there is even more to learn. Welcome to a whole new way of using this time-honored kitchen appliance. The slow cooker can be used to make caramelized vegetables, hot soufflés, and sophisticated game dishes. You can pair a slow cooker with an immersion blender to make rich, satiny-smooth creamless soups. You can use the slow cooker insert in the microwave oven to jump-start the cooking process and you can rely on the slow cooker to proof yeast dough and make sticky buns. Combine vegetable stock made in a slow cooker with caramelized onions to make a rich vegetarian onion soup, a low-fat vegetarian pasta sauce, or even caramelized onion risotto. Root vegetables roasted in the slow cooker are the base for an antipasto flavored with roasted garlic oil.

I recently taught at an upscale cooking school where I had promised to show thirty well-heeled men and women, perched attentively on their stools, the hippest, hottest thing to come on the culinary scene since precariously balanced vertical presentations. They watched with wide-eyed wonder as I reached down and, with a flourish, placed a slow cooker front and center on the work surface. "A slow cooker! Is she kidding?" There was a collective exhale of dismay as the class members gave each other the "for-this-I-paid-sixty-dollars?" look. As I lifted the lid off the homely appliance, a gentle billow of steam carried an aroma that was deeply and luxuriously redolent, buttery rich, and seductively alluring: whole Vidalia onions caramelized to a deep mahogany, flecked with bits of clove and bathed in double-rich Burgundy-based stock. Thirty noses moved from lofty disdain to hyperactive sniffing. "My God! What is that amazing smell?" As they leaned forward for a better look, I gave them an indulgent smile. "Today we'll be making cassoulet in the slow cooker," I announced. By the next day every member of the class owned a slow cooker.

Slow Cooker Basics

A slow cooker consists of a heavy-duty, glazed ceramic insert with a clear plastic or glass cover. This insert fits into a lightweight metal housing with an electric heating coil. When the coil is switched on, the insert absorbs the heat and gently cooks the food inside without allowing any moisture to escape. I prefer the slow cookers that come with a dishwasher- and microwave-safe removable insert that can be placed in the oven or the refrigerator.

All the recipes in this book were tested using Rival Crock-Pots®. I prefer this brand because the appliance is nationally available, affordable, reliable, and sturdy. The heat is conducted evenly, and the outside metal housing doesn't get as hot as some other brands. Crock-Pot® is a registered trademark of the Rival company. All Crock-Pots® are made by Rival, but not all slow cookers are Crock-Pots®. Crock-Pots® can be found in department, houseware, and hardware stores. They come in solid colors that are much more attractive (to my taste) than the traditional flowers, grapes, or dancing vegetables motifs.

Different machines may cook at different temperatures, so if you are using a brand other than Rival, it is especially important to check each dish for doneness. In fact, even when using the same brand as I did, it's important to check. There are three ways. The first is visual: Does it look done? Is it golden brown or as soft as it should be? The second is textural: Does a knife pierce the food easily? Is the interior of the meat, fish, or poultry cooked through? The third is taste: Are the flavors fully developed? (The food should not taste raw or undercooked.)

My team of testers used slow cookers of varying sizes, from the smallest, which holds about 3 cups, to the 5½-quart oval, which quickly became my favorite. Although it's not necessary to own more than two sizes, you might consider having a smaller (3- to 4-quart) model for chutneys, sauces, and recipes that feed about 4 people, and a large machine, such as the 5½-quart, for entertaining.

Time, money, and energy are precious commodities. Imagine an appliance that promises to save you all three, and then delivers. You put the ingredients into the machine, and that's it. No more standing around, poking your head in the oven to see if the dish is cooked. No more heating up the kitchen or getting the oven dirty. No more using and washing multiple pots and pans. You can let the slow cooker make dinner while you sleep, work, run errands, or go to the gym. If you're running late, don't worry: In most cases, an extra hour of cooking time won't make much difference. I have used slow cookers for years, and I have left them on all night or all day long. While testing these recipes, I had an average of four slow cookers going at one time, often around the clock, and never, ever had any kind of electrical problem as a result. If you are concerned about leaving an electric appliance on while you are sleeping or away, then follow your instincts and use it only while you are home and awake.

Slow cookers are synonymous with one-pot meals. Although there are such recipes in this book, I've also included pantry recipes, which become key ingredients in other dishes. There's a recipe for duxelles, a preparation of finely chopped, slowly simmered mushrooms, which can be used as a stuffing for large mushroom caps or as a spread for crostini. The Pear Anise Purée (page 18) becomes a base for a soufflé and a sorbet.

Once you've placed ingredients in the slow cooker and turned it on, it is neither necessary nor advisable to lift the lid to stir the mixture. The steam generated in the cooking creates a vacuum that seals the lid. Every time you open the lid, both steam and heat dissipate, which can prolong the cooking time. Several recipes do instruct you to stir halfway through the cooking time or toward the end, but unless instructed to do so, it's best to leave the lid in place.

Take care not to fill the insert so much that the lid doesn't fit tightly. Without a tight fit a vacuum will not form, which will dramatically affect cooking time.

Avoid placing a hot insert directly onto a very cold surface. There is a remote possibility that the shock will make it crack.

It's very important to clean the insert completely between uses. Built-up food stains are impossible to remove. I often put the inserts in the dishwasher.

When cooking at a high altitude, be sure to allow an additional 30 minutes for each hour of cooking time specified in the recipe. Legumes, in particular, take twice as long to cook at a high altitude as at sea level. At any altitude, cooking on LOW heat generally—but not always—takes about twice as long as cooking on HIGH.

Because things cook for a long time, I usually note the time I turn on the slow cooker on a piece of paper and put it on the counter. It is sometimes advisable to use a thermometer to test for doneness. The ideal one, made by Polder, consists of a metal probe connected by a thin metal filament to a plastic base with a timer and a digital temperature readout. You program for the desired temperature, and the timer goes off when it is reached. You can insert the probe in the food and run the metal filament out of the pot with the top in place; a vacuum will still be formed. This works best if your slow cooker has a glass lid.

Because there is no evaporation during cooking, there may be excess liquid in the insert at the end of the cooking time. If so, drain it into a small saucepan and simmer until it has reduced to an appropriate amount. It's important to add seasonings after this reduction takes place, rather than before, since reducing the liquid will intensify the taste.

Condensation will form in the lid. To avoid dripping the condensation onto the food, always lift the lid gently, straight up, without tilting it, until it is away from the insert.

In addition to its usual position in the electric base, the slow cooker's heavy ceramic insert can be used in the microwave, in the oven, and under the broiler. This makes it easy to soften or even brown onions and garlic in the microwave before you add ingredients for stews, soups, and sauces. You can freeze food right in the ceramic insert and defrost it by placing the insert directly in the microwave. (But don't use the plugged-in slow cooker to defrost frozen food.) Top a finished dish with bread crumbs, biscuit batter, yeast dough, streusel, or mashed potatoes, and then place the insert in the oven or under the broiler to bake, brown, or crisp. Sprinkle cheese over savory dishes or powdered sugar over desserts and run them under the broiler until the topping has melted or caramelized.

Browning meat and some cuts of poultry before placing them in the slow cooker adds immensely to the finished flavor. Dredging them in flour before browning thickens the cooking liquid into a sauce that needs only to be skimmed of fat and seasoned before serving. While some foods will brown during the cooking process (particularly if they are not submerged in liquid), they will not develop the same color and flavor that they get when browned first on the stove top. If you can find the time for this step, the results will be worth the effort.

Pantry

Chicken Stock

YIELD: 8 cups stock

COOKING TIME: 6 to 8 hours on HIGH

SLOW COOKER SIZE: 5½ quart

1 (4-pound) chicken, or
4 pounds chicken parts

2 medium onions, peeled and
quartered

2 medium carrots, peeled and
cut crosswise into thirds

2 medium parsnips, peeled and
cut crosswise into thirds

2 celery stalks, washed and cut
crosswise into thirds

2 bay leaves

8 whole cloves

8 black peppercorns

3 garlic cloves, unpeeled and
halved

Pinch each dried rosemary,
thyme, and basil, or 2 sprigs of
each fresh herb

8 cups water

GOOD CHICKEN STOCK IS THE BASIS FOR SO many recipes. While canned broth will do, nothing beats the homemade kind.

Rinse the chicken. If you are using a whole chicken, discard the bag of giblets from the cavity. Place the chicken in the insert of the slow cooker. Add the onions, carrots, parsnips, celery, bay leaves, cloves, peppercorns, garlic, and herbs. If there isn't enough room, stuff some of the vegetables into the chicken cavity. Add as much of the water as the insert will allow. Cover and cook on HIGH for 6 to 8 hours. The meat will be falling off the bones.

Turn the slow cooker off and let the stock cool, uncovered, for about 1 hour. Strain the stock through a fine-mesh sieve or a sieve lined with cheesecloth into a metal bowl. Discard the chicken carcass and vegetables. Refrigerate the stock. It will be easy to remove the fat after it has congealed on the top. (You might want to save it for Chopped Liver, page 31.) Use the stock within 3 days, or freeze it in covered plastic containers for up to 6 months.

Vegetable Stock

YIELD: 8 cups

COOKING TIME: 6 hours on HIGH

SLOW COOKER SIZE: 4 quart

2 medium onions, peeled and cut into 1/2-inch-thick slices

2 large celery stalks, cut into 1/2-inch-thick slices

2 large carrots, peeled and cut into 1/2-inch-thick slices

1 small bulb fresh fennel, rough base and leafy stalks discarded (save some fronds for stock), bulb cut lengthwise into 1/2-inch-thick slices

2 large leeks, roots and all but 4 inches of green leaves discarded, leeks quartered and well rinsed

1 large sweet green pepper, seeds and membranes discarded, and cut into 1/2-inch-strips

4 unpeeled garlic cloves, crushed

2 tablespoons vegetable oil

6 sprigs fresh flat-leaf parsley

6 sprigs fresh thyme

1 large bay leaf

6 whole black peppercorns

6 reserved leafy fronds from the fennel stalks

10 cups water

1 1/2 teaspoons salt

THIS FLAVORFUL STOCK WILL ADD A DEPTH OF flavor to soups, stews, and sauces. Roasting the vegetables before they are added to the slow cooker brings out the sweetness in the root vegetables and gives the broth a beautiful amber hue.

Preheat the oven to 450°F with a rack at the center position. Line a large, shallow heavy-duty baking pan with aluminum foil.

Place the onions, celery, carrots, fennel, leeks, green pepper, and garlic on the lined baking pan and drizzle with the vegetable oil. Toss the vegetables to coat them with the oil and roast them in the oven for 30 minutes. Remove the pan from the oven to stir the vegetables after the first 15 minutes.

While the vegetables are roasting, place the parsley, thyme, bay leaf, peppercorns, and fennel fronds in a piece of cheesecloth and tie securely. When the vegetables are lightly browned around the edges, scrape them with any accumulated juices into the insert if the slow cooker. Bury the cheesecloth bag among the vegetables, pour in the water, and add the salt. Cover and cook on HIGH for 6 hours, until the stock is bubbling, the vegetables are very soft, and the stock is a deep amber color.

Turn the slow cooker off and let the stock cool slightly. Strain the stock into a bowl. Press hard on the vegetables and cheesecloth bag, then discard them. Store the stock in covered containers in the refrigerator for 1 week, or freeze for up to 6 months.

Caramelized Onions

Yield: about 3½ cups

Cooking time: 12 to 14 hours on LOW

Slow cooker size: 4 quart

3 pounds Vidalia or other sweet onions (4 to 5 onions, 3 to 4 inches in diameter), peeled and cut into ⅛-inch-thick to ¼-inch-thick slices

8 tablespoons (1 stick) butter (see Note)

This recipe made me fall in love with my slow cooker and recognize its potential for dishes other than beef stew and chili. Caramelizing onions in the slow cooker eliminates the possibility of burning them that exists when you cook them on the stove top. An added bonus is the heady broth you end up with, which can be used in other dishes along with the onions.

Use the onions and liquid to flavor soups, stocks, and stews. They make a wonderful addition to risotto, a perfect pasta sauce, and the world's best pizza topping (for this use you will have to drain off the liquid first). The onions can be served on their own as a vegetable to accompany fish, meat, or fowl. Cook a very long time until they are a deep mahogany color.

Place the onions and butter in the insert of the slow cooker, cover, and cook on LOW for 12 to 14 hours, until the onions are deep brown and very soft. It's almost impossible to overcook these; make sure to let the onions cook until they are mahogany colored.

Notes: While this recipe calls for Vidalia onions, you can use other sweet onions such as Maui, Walla Walla, or Texas 1015s. If you have a large slow cooker, you can double the onions. It is not necessary to increase the amount of butter.

Don't blanch at the amount of butter called for here. When you drain and chill the onions, the onion-flavored butter will congeal on the surface of the cooking liquid. Skim it and use it when you sauté other vegetables, over pasta, or in risotto.

Duxelles

YIELD: about 3 cups

COOKING TIME: 8 to 12 hours on HIGH

SIZE SLOW COOKER: 4 quart

2½ pounds cultivated white mushrooms, cleaned, stems trimmed, thinly sliced (slicing can be done in the food processor)

3 large shallots, peeled and minced

1 stick (8 tablespoons) butter

½ teaspoon salt

Freshly ground black pepper

IT USED TO TAKE HOURS OF STIRRING AND HOVER-ing over the stove to prepare this classic French savory paste of finely chopped mushrooms and shallots. While the cooking time has increased, the stirring and hovering has been eliminated, thanks to the slow cooker. Use Duxelles to make Duxelles-Stuffed Mushrooms (page 29) or add them to Risotto with Parmesan (page 160).

Place the mushrooms, shallots, and butter in the insert of the slow cooker. Cover and cook on HIGH for at least 8 hours, until the mushrooms are very soft. Turn off the slow cooker and let the mushrooms cool slightly.

Pour the mushrooms and liquid into a strainer placed over a bowl. Save the cooking liquid.

Transfer the mushrooms to the work bowl of a food processor. Pulse until the pieces are very small, but don't let the mixture become a smooth purée. Stir in the salt and pepper to taste.

Store the puréed mushrooms and their liquid separately. Some recipes that call for duxelles also require some of the liquid. The cooking liquid can be used on its own to enrich soups, stews, sauces, and risotto.

Place the duxelles in small resealable plastic bags and the juice in tightly covered containers. Store both in the refrigerator for up to 2 weeks, or in the freezer for up to 6 months.

Braised Chestnuts

YIELD: 6 cups shelled chestnut meat

COOKING TIME: 5 hours on HIGH

SLOW COOKER SIZE: 4 to 6 quart

3 pounds fresh chestnuts, carefully picked over to avoid those with worm holes or mold

Boiling water to cover the chestnuts

FRESH CHESTNUTS APPEAR IN MARKETS DURING the fall—just in time for Thanksgiving stuffing and fancy Christmas desserts like Mont Blanc. Canned chestnuts don't begin to measure up in flavor and texture to fresh ones. The problem with fresh chestnuts, however, is that it is a pain to remove the hard outer shell and the thin peel stubbornly attached to the nut. One rather unsatisfactory method is to roast them in an inch or two of water, then burn your fingers as you try to peel them while still hot.

The best way I've found so far is this slow cooker method. You have a good deal of flexibility in the cooking time, and the chestnuts stay warm enough to peel without burning you. If you want your chestnuts to be in large pieces, then use the shorter cooking time; otherwise, let them cook until they are quite soft. The result will be tasty crumbles that can be used in Chestnut, Cranberry, and Corn Muffin Bread Pudding (page 158), Cream of Chestnut Soup (page 64), and Candied Chestnuts in Syrup (page 20).

Place each chestnut flat side down on a work surface and use a heavy, sharp chef's knife, a 1-inch chisel and a hammer, or a chestnut knife to cut a deep slit that extends at least halfway through the chestnut. (If you accidentally cut some nuts in half, it's all right.) Place the chestnuts in the slow cooker, add the water, cover, and cook on HIGH for at least 2½ hours and up to 5 hours, or until the shells have begun to curl back and the meat is slightly tender. Reduce the slow cooker heat to LOW.

If you have them, it's best to wear a pair of thin rubber (surgical) gloves when you peel the chestnuts, as they are very drying and will irritate your hands. Remove one chestnut at a time from the slow cooker, and then replace the lid. Place the chestnut on a work surface and use a chef's knife to cut it in half. Squeeze each piece of shell so that the meat falls out. Use a butter knife with a rounded end to scrape out any lingering meat, trying not to dislodge the thin dark inner peel as you do so. As you remove the meat, check for moldy, rotten, or wormy nuts, and discard them. The chestnut meat can be stored in heavy-duty resealable plastic bags in the refrigerator for up to 3 days, or in the freezer for up to 3 months.

Frijoles Negros (Black Beans)

YIELD: about 8 cups

COOKING TIME: 12 to 18 hours on HIGH

SLOW COOKER SIZE: 5 quart

1 pound dried black (turtle) beans, rinsed, drained, and picked over to remove any bits of dirt and debris

1 cup loosely packed fresh cilantro leaves

1 large onion, peeled and chopped

3 garlic cloves, peeled and minced

10 cups low-sodium chicken broth, vegetable broth, Chicken Stock (page 8), or Vegetable Stock (page 9)

⅓ cup vegetable oil

1 smoked ham hock or ½ pound smoked turkey cut into 1-inch cubes, optional

Tabasco, optional

Salt and freshly ground black pepper

IT'S A STEW. IT'S A SOUP. IT'S A VEGETABLE. IT'S A vegetarian's idea of heaven. Black beans are a staple in Mexican and Southwestern cooking, and preparing them in the slow cooker is so easy that there's no excuse not to have them on hand to enjoy in dozens of preparations. Overcooking this dish is virtually impossible, thus the big range of cooking times.

Place the beans, cilantro, onion, garlic, broth, oil, and the optional meat in the insert of the slow cooker. Cover, and cook on HIGH for 12 to 18 hours, or until the beans are extremely soft.

Add the optional Tabasco and salt and pepper to taste.

Serve as is with rice, or use in Black Bean Dip (page 38), Black Bean Soup (page 59), Refried Beans (page 84), and Black Bean Bread (page 153).

Slow Cooked Chickpeas

YIELD: 6 cups

COOKING TIME: 6 to 8 hours on HIGH

SLOW COOKER SIZE: 5½ quart

1 pound dried chickpeas, rinsed, drained, and picked over to remove any bits of dirt and debris

6 cups water, low-sodium chicken broth, or Chicken Stock (page 8)

1 teaspoon salt

Freshly ground black pepper

COOKED CHICKPEAS ARE USED IN MANY RECIPES from many cuisines. They appear in Indian curries, Spanish soups, Lebanese stews, and Middle Eastern salads. Starting with dried chickpeas is vastly better than using canned ones. The nutty, almost sweet taste of cooked chickpeas (*garbanzos* in Spanish) sings out loud and clear; wait till you taste the Hummus on page 26.

Place the chickpeas and water in the insert of the slow cooker. Cover and cook on HIGH for 6 hours, or until the chickpeas are tender when cut or mashed. Add the salt and pepper to taste. Drain and use as desired.

Rosemary-Infused Oil

YIELD: 1 cup

COOKING TIME: 1½ to 2 hours on HIGH

SLOW COOKER SIZE: 4 quart

1 cup mild olive oil or vegetable oil

¼ cup packed chopped fresh rosemary leaves

I LOVE ROSEMARY-INFUSED OIL FOR STIRRING INTO soup, for drizzling on pasta and vegetables, and for dipping with good Italian bread. When I've made it in the past on my stove top, it was hard to keep the oil in a small saucepan from getting too hot too fast. Those days are over. I can't believe how wonderful the slow cooker is for making this versatile addition to the year-round pantry. The finished infusion is a lovely pale green, and your kitchen will smell like Provence.

Place the oil and the rosemary in the insert of the slow cooker. Cook on HIGH, *uncovered,* for 1½ to 2 hours, and then turn the slow cooker off. Allow the oil to cool for about 20 minutes, and then pour it through a sieve lined with a clean paper towel or paper coffee filter into a metal bowl. When the oil is completely cool, transfer it to a clean glass jar, cover, and refrigerate for up to 1 month; after that the flavor may fade. The oil may cloud under refrigeration, but it will become clear again at room temperature.

VARIATION: Basil-Infused Oil: Proceed as for Rosemary-Infused Oil, using 1 cup of oil and ⅓ to ½ cup of packed roughly chopped fresh basil leaves. Strain and store as for Rosemary-Infused Oil.

Golden Tomato Sauce

YIELD: 2 quarts

COOKING TIME: 6 to 7 hours on LOW or 4 hours on HIGH

SLOW COOKER SIZE: 5½ to 6 quart

¼ cup olive oil

4 garlic cloves, peeled and minced

2 large sweet onions (such as Maui or Vidalia), peeled and chopped, or 2 cups Caramelized Onions (page 10)

¼ cup packed brown sugar

¼ cup balsamic vinegar

2 tablespoons honey

1 tablespoon salt

2 pounds large golden tomatoes, seeded and chopped

2 large yellow bell peppers, cored, seeded, and cut into 1-inch pieces

½ cup low-sodium chicken broth, vegetable broth, Chicken Stock (page 8), or Vegetable Stock (page 9)

2 tablespoons fresh oregano leaves

Freshly ground black pepper

LARGE, SUCCULENT TOMATOES, THE SIZE OF small grapefruits and the color of yellow bell peppers, can be found in farmer's markets in late summer. This sauce is perfect as a topping for pasta, stirred into hot risotto, or as a bright-colored sauce over fish. You can even purée it with additional vegetable or chicken broth, and then chill it to make a fabulous cold summer soup.

Heat the olive oil in a large sauté pan set over medium heat and cook the garlic until light golden brown. Use a slotted spoon to transfer the garlic to the slow cooker. If you are using raw onions, add them to the pan and cook, stirring frequently, until golden brown. Scrape them into the insert of the slow cooker, and then add the brown sugar, vinegar, honey, salt, tomatoes, bell peppers, broth, oregano, and pepper to taste. Cover and cook on LOW for 6 to 7 hours or on HIGH for 3 to 4 hours, until the vegetables are very soft. If you are using caramelized onions, stir them into the hot tomato sauce at the end of the cooking time, then cover the insert and allow the onions to heat through.

Mash the sauce with a hand-held potato masher to create a chunky sauce. Taste and season with additional salt and pepper, if desired.

Pear Anise Purée

YIELD: 5 cups

COOKING TIME: 4 to 6 hours on HIGH

SLOW COOKER SIZE: 4 quart

4 large, ripe, flavorful Comice or Anjou pears, halved, cored, and cut into 1-inch chunks

¼ cup anisette or Poire William

Finely grated zest and strained juice of 1 lemon

1 cup granulated sugar

THIS MAKES A PERFECT BASE FOR A DESSERT soufflé (page 166), a sorbet (page 168), or a sauce for a pear tart. Poire William, a pear-flavored eau-de-vie, can be substituted for the anisette if you do not want a licorice flavor.

Place the pears, anisette, lemon zest and juice, and sugar in the insert of the slow cooker. Cover and cook on HIGH for at least 4 hours, or until the pears are soft. Cool slightly, and then use a slotted spoon to transfer the pears to a blender or food processor. Blend or pulse for 10 to 15 seconds, or just until the pears are mushy. With the blender or processor running, slowly pour in enough of the cooking liquid to make a thick purée. Store the rest of the cooking liquid for other uses, such as drizzling over fresh fruit or sorbet.

Triple Applesauce

YIELD: 4 to 5 cups

COOKING TIME: 5 to 6 hours on LOW or 3 hours on HIGH

SLOW COOKER SIZE: 3 quart

6 large, firm, flavorful apples (such as Fuji, Cortland, Baldwin, or Granny Smith), stemmed and quartered (see Note)

1½ cups dried apple rings, each ring cut into 4 pieces

⅓ cup granulated sugar

Finely grated zest and strained juice of 1 large lemon

1 cup apple cider

1 cinnamon stick

½ teaspoon ground nutmeg

½ teaspoon ground cloves

½ teaspoon ground ginger

FRESH APPLES, DRIED APPLES, AND APPLE CIDER combine to make a fragrant dish that is perfect alone or as a condiment for potato pancakes or roast meat or game. It is the base for Triple Applesauce Granita (page 170). I cook red-skinned apples with the skins on because it gives more flavor and imparts a lovely color. A food mill comes in handy here; it allows you to strain out the seeds and skins as you purée the cooked fruit.

Place the apples, dried apple rings, sugar, lemon zest and juice, cider, cinnamon stick, nutmeg, cloves, and ginger in the slow cooker insert. Cover and cook on LOW for 5 to 6 hours or on HIGH for 3 hours, until the apples are very tender.

Discard the cinnamon stick and use a slotted spoon to transfer the apple solids to a food mill or a food processor. Purée them, and add enough cooking juices to achieve the desired consistency.

Serve the applesauce warm or cold by itself, or as an accompaniment to meat or game dishes.

NOTE: If you are using a food processor to purée the fruit, core and seed the apples before you cook them.

Candied Chestnuts in Syrup

YIELD: 2 cups

COOKING TIME: 8 to 12 hours on HIGH for candying the chestnuts; $2\frac{1}{2}$ to 5 hours for the braised chestnuts (an ingredient)

SLOW COOKER SIZE: 1 quart

2 cups peeled, crumbled chestnuts from Braised Chestnuts (page 12)

1 cup granulated sugar

½ cup water

⅓ cup dark rum

THESE ARE AN ESSENTIAL INGREDIENT IN MONT Blanc (page 177)—one of the world's most sophisticated desserts, which I somehow associate with Christmas dinner (but don't wait till then to serve it!). They also flavor Chestnut Ice Cream (page 172), and they form the center and sauce for a wonderful Chocolate Chestnut Soufflé (page 178).

Place the chestnuts, sugar, water, and rum in the insert of the slow cooker. Cover and cook on HIGH for 8 to 12 hours, or until the chestnuts are tender. Use a spoon to pick out any stray bits of peel. Use the candied nuts immediately, or refrigerate them in their syrup in a covered container for 1 week, or freeze for up to 6 months.

VARIATION: You can purée the candied chestnuts and store the purée so that it's ready to use for desserts such as Mont Blanc (page 177). When the candied nuts are cooked, drain the liquid into a spouted measuring cup and reserve it. Place the chestnuts in the bowl of a food processor and process for 20 to 30 seconds, or until no large pieces remain. With the processor running, pour some of the reserved liquid slowly through the feed tube and process until the mixture is the consistency of soft applesauce. (You may not need to use all the liquid.) The purée will thicken as it cools. Use the purée immediately, or scrape it into a plastic container. Cover securely and refrigerate for up to 1 week, or freeze for up to 6 months.

Dulce de Leche

YIELD: about 2 cups

COOKING TIME: about 10 hours on HIGH

SLOW COOKER SIZE: 4 quart

1 vanilla bean, split lengthwise

4 cups whole milk

1⅔ cups granulated sugar

¼ cup water

Large pinch baking soda

IF YOU HAVE BEEN HESITATING TO BUY A SLOW cooker and wanted a really great reason to push you over the fence, here it is! Food writer Victoria Abbot Riccardi described Dulce de Leche, a Latin American confection, in the *Boston Globe*: "Like toffee, butterscotch, and honey all rolled into one, this thick tawny ambrosia consists of whole milk, sugar, and vanilla slowly cooked into a sticky jam." Well, Victoria, I couldn't have possibly said it any better myself. As soon as I read that, I was hooked. When I read Victoria's directions, which cautioned that the mixture had to be stirred and carefully watched to avoid burning, I realized this would be perfect for the slow cooker—and it is! As the milk and sugar slowly caramelize, the kitchen—and soon your entire home—fills with the intoxicating aroma of something seriously good to eat.

Although you can eat the cooled mixture right out of the insert, I suggest you pour it over ice cream, fruit, or cake, or mix it into coffee. Or try Dulce de Leche Whipped Cream or Ice Cream (page 174) or Marbled Cheesecake with Dulce de Leche (page 181)—three amazing desserts.

Place the vanilla bean, 3 cups of the milk, the sugar, water, and baking soda in the insert of the slow cooker, and whisk them together. Cook for 9 hours on HIGH, *uncovered,* then remove the vanilla bean and whisk the milk mixture gently. Use a dull-edged butter knife to carefully scrape down the crust of sugar that accumulates on the sides of the insert. Do not skim the foam off the top of the mixture.

Continue cooking for 1 more hour, stirring every 20 minutes, until it is a rich medium-caramel color and has thickened to the consistency of melted ice cream. In the meantime, warm the remaining 1 cup of milk in a small saucepan. Turn off the slow cooker, and stir in the warm milk. (This will prevent the dulce de leche from hardening while refrigerated.) Carefully remove the insert. Allow the mixture to cool for 10 minutes, then spoon and scrape it into a small metal bowl. Cover and cool to room temperature. The mixture will thicken slightly as it cools. Refrigerate it in a tightly covered container for up to 3 months.

Appetizers

Tomatillo Salsa
with Peppers

YIELD: about 6 cups

COOKING TIME: $1\frac{1}{2}$ to 2 hours on HIGH;
longer cooking causes the colors of the vegetables to fade.

SLOW COOKER SIZE: $2\frac{1}{2}$ quart

¼ cup plus 3 tablespoons olive oil

6 medium shallots, peeled and minced

4 garlic cloves, peeled and finely chopped

1 pound fresh tomatillos (see Note), outer skin removed, cut in half

1 large red bell pepper, seeded and cut into 1-inch pieces

1 large yellow bell pepper, seeded and cut into 1-inch pieces

1 large orange bell pepper, seeded and cut into 1-inch pieces

¼ cup chopped fresh cilantro

⅓ cup tomato paste

¼ cup water

1 dried chipotle pepper, seeded and cut into very small pieces; or 1 canned chipotle in adobo sauce, seeded and minced (see Note)

THE LITTLE GREEN TOMATO-LIKE TOMATILLOS are an ancient fruit favored by the Aztecs and native to Mexico. They come "gift wrapped" in a delicate, papery husk and average one to two inches in diameter. Tart and hard even when ripe, these aren't very good uncooked, but they are lovely in recipes just like this one, which brings out their sweetness. This tricolored salsa is great with corn chips, in Fish Roulades with Tomatillo Salsa (page 148), or on the Tomatillo Salsa Pizza (page 161).

Heat ¼ cup of the olive oil in a small sauté pan over medium heat and sauté the shallots until they have softened. Scrape them into the insert of the slow cooker. (If your microwave oven is large enough to hold the slow cooker insert, place the oil and shallots in the insert, cover with the inverted lid or a flat plate, and place the insert in the microwave.) Cook on HIGH for 4 to 5 minutes, or until the shallots have softened.

Place the remaining ingredients, including the 3 tablespoons of oil, in the slow cooker insert. Cover and cook on HIGH for $1\frac{1}{2}$ to 2 hours, or until the vegetables are soft but not mushy. Serve with corn chips. The salsa can be stored in the refrigerator in a covered container for up to 2 weeks.

1 teaspoon smoked paprika
(see Note), or mild chili powder

1½ teaspoons salt

NOTES: Tomatillos are available in some grocery stores and in Latino markets. Dried chipotle peppers or chipotles in adobo sauce and smoked paprika can be found in specialty food stores. Smoked paprika is made from red peppers that are smoked with oak wood and then ground, giving the product a very distinct, smoky flavor. Look for La Chinata brand, which comes sweet, bittersweet, and hot.

Hummus

YIELD: 2½ cups

COOKING TIME: 5 minutes for the onions; 6 to 8 hours for the chickpeas

1 tablespoon olive oil, plus more if needed

1 large onion, peeled and minced

2 garlic cloves, peeled and minced

2 cups Slow Cooked Chickpeas (page 15), drained

½ cup strained fresh lemon juice (about 2 large lemons)

1 tablespoon soy sauce

¼ cup tahini (sesame paste)

Salt to taste

½ cup sesame seeds, toasted (see Note)

THIS TRADITIONAL MIDDLE EASTERN SPREAD IS made from ground chickpeas and tahini, or sesame paste, which can be found in the natural foods section of most supermarkets. Home-cooked chickpeas taste much better than the canned variety and will certainly make a difference in this recipe.

Heat 1 tablespoon of olive oil in a medium sauté pan over medium heat. Cook the onion and garlic until soft. Scrape them into the work bowl of a food processor fitted with a metal blade or into a blender. Add the chickpeas, lemon juice, soy sauce, and tahini. Process the mixture until quite smooth. Add more olive oil if the mixture is too thick. Taste, and add salt if needed. Scrape the hummus into a serving bowl and refrigerate until ready to use. Sprinkle the sesame seeds over the top of the hummus and serve as a dip for pita bread or fresh vegetables. Covered and refrigerated the hummus will keep for 1 month.

NOTE: To toast sesame seeds, place them in a small sauté pan over medium heat. Cook, stirring frequently, just until the seeds are light golden brown and fragrant. Remove them from the heat immediately because they burn easily.

Warm Chickpea Salad

YIELD: 6 servings

COOKING TIME: 6 to 8 hours for the chickpeas

FOR THE DRESSING

¼ cup balsamic vinegar

⅓ cup olive oil

2 tablespoons Dijon mustard

2 tablespoons soy sauce

FOR THE SALAD

3 cups hot Slow Cooked Chickpeas (page 15)

1 red onion, peeled and finely chopped

2 celery stalks, with leaves, finely diced

6 cups baby spinach leaves, well rinsed and patted dry

⅓ cup chopped fresh flat-leaf parsley

Salt and freshly ground black pepper

2 (4-ounce) cans Italian tuna in oil, partially drained and flaked

USE FRESHLY MADE SLOW COOKED CHICKPEAS (page 15) while they're still hot to prepare this satisfying salad right in the slow cooker insert.

Combine the dressing ingredients in a small mixing bowl. Whisk well and set aside.

To the hot chickpeas in the slow cooker insert add the onion, celery, spinach, parsley, and salt and pepper to taste. Toss the salad ingredients together, add some of the dressing, and toss again. Divide among 6 salad plates, and top each serving with some of the tuna. Drizzle on more dressing if desired.

Sherried Duxelles Spread

YIELD: 1 generous cup

COOKING TIME: 8 to 12 hours for the duxelles

1 cup Duxelles (page 11), drained

2 tablespoons butter, softened and cut into 4 pieces

1½ teaspoons chopped fresh chives

1 teaspoon fresh thyme leaves

¼ cup heavy cream

3 to 4 tablespoons dry or medium-dry sherry

Salt and freshly ground black pepper

Toast points or crackers

ONCE THE SLOW COOKER HAS DONE THE WORK of making the Duxelles (page 11), use this easy recipe and your food processor to make a simple but elegant spread.

Put the duxelles, butter, chives, and thyme leaves in a food processor fitted with the metal blade, and pulse until the mixture is finely ground. With the motor running, pour the cream and 3 tablespoons of sherry through the feed tube. Process until the mixture is a smooth purée. Taste, add more sherry, if desired, and salt and pepper to taste. Spoon the spread into a ramekin and serve with toast points or crackers.

Duxelles-Stuffed Mushrooms

YIELD: 12 stuffed caps

COOKING TIME: 25 to 30 minutes to bake the mushrooms;
8 to 12 hours for the duxelles

12 white mushrooms caps, 2 to 2½ inches in diameter, cleaned

1 tablespoon butter

¾ cup fresh bread crumbs, preferably from firm-textured French or Italian bread

2 shallots, peeled and finely chopped

⅓ cup finely chopped pancetta or smoked bacon (about 1½ ounces)

1 cup Duxelles (page 11), drained

½ teaspoon finely chopped fresh rosemary

Salt and freshly ground black pepper

3 to 4 tablespoons Duxelles cooking liquid, low-sodium chicken broth, or Chicken Stock (page 8), if needed

3 to 4 tablespoons freshly grated cheese, preferably Parmigiano-Reggiano

IF YOU ARE LOOKING FOR AN EASY BUT ELEGANT passed appetizer, then this is the recipe for you. You can bake the mushrooms as much as 24 hours ahead of time, and then cover and refrigerate them. Serve at room temperature, or rewarm them, covered, in a 350°F oven until just heated through.

Preheat the oven to 375°F with a rack in the center position. Line a heavy-duty rimmed baking sheet or shallow roasting pan with aluminum foil.

To enlarge the stuffing cavity, use a small spoon to gently scrape out some of the mushroom flesh in each cap where the stem was attached. Set the mushrooms aside.

Heat ½ tablespoon of butter in a heavy, medium sauté pan over medium-high heat. Toss the bread crumbs in the butter and cook, stirring, until lightly browned, about 4 minutes. Scrape them into a medium mixing bowl.

Melt the remaining ½ tablespoon of butter in the sauté pan over medium-high heat and cook the shallots until they have softened, about 4 minutes. Add the pancetta or bacon and cook, stirring, over medium heat for 5 minutes more. Scrape the shallot mixture into the mixing bowl containing the bread crumbs, and then stir in the duxelles, rosemary, and salt and freshly ground black pepper to taste. If the mixture seems dry, stir in some of the duxelles cooking liquid. Taste for seasoning.

Lightly salt the mushroom cavities. Mound the stuffing mixture generously in each cap, pressing gently on the stuffing. Place the caps, stuffing side up, on the baking sheet. Sprinkle the top of each stuffed mushroom generously with cheese. Bake for 25 to 30 minutes, until the stuffing is hot and the mushroom caps have softened slightly. Serve hot or warm.

Chopped Liver

Yield: about 3 cups

Cooking time: 1 hour on HIGH

Slow cooker size: 2 to 3 quart

3 to 4 tablespoons rendered chicken fat or butter (see Note)

1 large onion, peeled and finely chopped

2 garlic cloves, peeled and minced

1 pound chicken livers, rinsed and patted dry

½ teaspoon dried thyme

Kosher salt and freshly ground black pepper

red onion slices

If you're Jewish, you might serve this on Friday night, on Rosh Hashanah, Passover, and at the break-fast meal after sundown on Yom Kippur. If you're not Jewish, you don't have to wait for a holiday. It's delicious spread on rye bread with a side of chicken fat sprinkled with coarse salt and freshly ground black pepper. Don't forget the sliced red onion!

Heat the chicken fat or butter in a small sauté pan over medium-high heat and sauté the chopped onion until golden brown. Reduce the heat to medium, add the garlic, and cook for another 2 minutes without allowing the garlic to brown. Scrape the mixture into the insert of the slow cooker. (If your microwave oven is large enough to hold the slow cooker insert, place the chicken fat or butter, the chopped onion, and garlic in the insert of the slow cooker. Cover with the inverted lid or a flat plate, place the insert in the microwave, and cook on HIGH for 4 to 5 minutes, or until the onions and garlic have softened.)

Place the chicken livers and thyme in the insert and stir to combine them with the onion and garlic. Cover and cook on HIGH for 1 hour, or until the outsides of the livers are dark and the insides are just slightly pink. Drain the accumulated cooking liquid into a small saucepan. Set it over high heat and reduce by two thirds.

Chop the livers with a chef's knife and place them in a bowl, adding some of the reduced cooking liquid, if necessary, for the proper consistency. (The livers may be chopped in a food processor fitted with the metal blade. Pulse the livers, add some of the reduced cooking liquid, if necessary, for the proper consistency, and pulse again.) Taste and add salt and freshly ground pepper. Serve, garnished with red onion slices, with crackers or rye bread.

NOTE: There are three ways to get chicken fat for this recipe: You can skim congealed fat off the top of chicken soup or stock, buy it in a plastic tub from a kosher butcher, or make it yourself. To make your own, place raw chicken fat in a small, heavy saucepan and cook very slowly over medium-low heat until the fat has melted, the connective tissue has darkened and crisped, and any water has evaporated. Strain the rendered fat into a bowl. Rendered chicken fat can be kept in a sealed container in the freezer for up to 6 months.

Truffle Shortcakes
with Salmon

YIELD: 9 shortcakes

COOKING TIME: 15 minutes for the shortcakes; 1½ hours for the salmon

FOR THE BISCUITS

¾ cup whole milk

1 tablespoon white vinegar

2 cups all-purpose flour

2 tablespoons Lora Brody's Dough Relaxer™, optional

2 teaspoons baking powder

½ teaspoon baking soda

½ teaspoon salt

1 tablespoon granulated sugar

8 tablespoons (1 stick) chilled unsalted butter, cut into small pieces

1 tablespoon white truffle oil (see Note)

FOR THE SALMON SHORTCAKES

1 recipe Slow Cooked Salmon (page 142), cooled

About 1 cup mascarpone cheese

Juice of 1 lemon, strained

Chopped fresh dill

I CAN'T THINK OF A MORE INDULGENT PRESENTA-tion of Slow Cooked Salmon (page 142) than this outrageously decadent and fabulously delectable first course.

Preheat the oven to 425°F with a rack in the center position. Line a heavy-duty baking sheet with aluminum foil or parchment paper. Measure the milk into a 1-cup spouted measure, and then add the vinegar. (The mixture will curdle.) Set aside.

Place a large mesh sieve over a medium mixing bowl and add the flour, optional Dough Relaxer, baking powder, baking soda, salt, and sugar. Shake the contents into the bowl. Scatter the butter pieces over the flour mixture and sprinkle the truffle oil over all. Use two butter knives in a crisscross motion to cut the butter into the flour until the mixture resembles coarse crumbs. Dribble in the milk mixture and stir the dough with a fork until it is sticky and just starts to hold together in a rough mass.

Turn the dough out onto a lightly floured work surface. Gently knead the dough with your hands into a smooth ball, giving it about 10 turns. Pat out the dough until it is about ½ inch thick. Use a 2-inch round cookie cutter to cut out 9 rounds. Gather the remaining dough and flatten it once again if necessary. Place the rounds 1½ inches apart on the prepared baking sheet. Bake for 14 to 16 minutes, or until the tops are lightly browned. Remove the biscuits to a wire rack to cool to room temperature.

To assemble the salmon shortcakes, first remove the bones from the salmon and use a fork to flake the fish into bite-size pieces. Use a serrated knife to split each biscuit in half. Place the bottom half of one biscuit, cut side up, on a plate, then spread the cut surface with a generous tablespoon of mascarpone cheese. Top with a serving of salmon, drizzle lightly with some lemon juice, and top with the other biscuit half. Garnish the top with a dab of mascarpone and a sprinkling of chopped dill. Repeat the process to make 8 more shortcakes.

NOTE: White truffle oil is available in gourmet stores and specialty markets.

Cheese Fondue

YIELD: 8 to 10 servings

COOKING TIME: 1 to 2 hours on HIGH

SLOW COOKER SIZE: 4 to 6 quart

¾ cup dry white wine

8 ounces Gruyère cheese, shredded

8 ounces Italian fontina cheese, shredded

2 tablespoons all-purpose flour

½ teaspoon dry mustard

Bite-size cubes of focaccia or French bread

FONDUE IS MAKING A COMEBACK, AND THERE'S no easier way to prepare it than in a slow cooker. Be sure to use genuine Gruyère cheese—the nutty taste is unique and "makes" the dish.

Pour the wine into the insert of the slow cooker. Turn the cooker on HIGH and warm the wine, *uncovered,* while you prepare the cheese.

Place the Gruyère, fontina, flour, and mustard in a gallon-size resealable plastic bag. Seal the bag carefully and shake vigorously until the contents are well mixed. There will be little or no trace of the flour.

When the wine is very warm, add about 1 cup of the cheese mixture to the wine and stir. Leave the insert uncovered, and when the first batch of cheese has melted, add another cup of the cheese mixture and stir. Continue in this way until all the cheese has melted and the wine is incorporated in the mixture.

Turn the slow cooker to LOW and serve. Fondue forks, wooden barbecue skewers, or table forks can be used to pierce the bread cubes and dip them into the cheese mixture.

Brandade

YIELD: about 6 cups

COOKING TIME: 9 hours on LOW or 5 hours on HIGH

SLOW COOKER SIZE: 4 to 5 quart

1 pound skinless, boneless salt cod

2 large Idaho potatoes, peeled and diced

4 tablespoons butter

1 large onion, peeled and diced

5 garlic cloves, peeled and minced

2 celery stalks, chopped

4 cups whole milk

1 rounded teaspoon dried *herbes de Provence* (see Note)

¼ cup olive oil

⅓ to ½ cup heavy cream

Sea salt and freshly ground black pepper

4 to 6 drops Tabasco

Rounds of toasted French bread

THIS VERSION OF BRANDADE, A SPECIALTY OF southern France made from salt cod, garlic, potatoes, and cream, is delicious on its own without the authentic touch of shaved black truffles. While most people consider this an appetizer, I like to add two over-easy fried eggs for a heavenly breakfast.

You'll find boned and filleted salt cod packed in wooden boxes, either with the frozen fish or in the fish case of your supermarket. Be sure to plan ahead with this dish; the cod needs to soak for 24 hours.

Defrost the salt cod, if necessary, and pick over the fish to remove any bones. Place the fish in a colander and rinse under cold running water for 10 minutes. Place the fish in a large bowl and cover with cold water. Cover the bowl and refrigerate for 24 hours, changing the water every 6 to 8 hours. Drain off and discard the water, place the fish on a cutting board, and rinse the bowl. Cut the fish into 2-inch pieces and set aside.

In the same bowl, place the potatoes and cover with cold water. Let the potatoes soak while you prepare the remaining ingredients.

Heat the butter in a medium sauté pan over medium heat and sauté the onion until soft and light golden brown. Add the garlic and celery and cook until the garlic is soft but not brown. Scrape the mixture into the insert of the slow cooker. (If your microwave oven is large enough to hold the slow cooker insert, place the butter, onion, garlic, and celery in the insert, cover with the inverted lid or a flat plate, place the insert in the microwave, and cook on HIGH for 4 to 5 minutes, or until the vegetables have softened. They will not get brown.)

Drain the potatoes and add them to the garlic and celery mixture in the slow cooker insert. Add the fish, milk, and *herbes de Provence* and stir to combine. Cover and cook on LOW for 9 hours or on HIGH for 5 hours, or until the potatoes are fork-tender. Use a slotted spoon to transfer half the mixture to the work bowl of a food processor fitted with the plastic blade. Discard any cooking liquid. Pulse to blend, and then, with the motor running, add half the olive oil and enough of the heavy cream to form a soft mixture like mashed potatoes. Do not overprocess, because the potatoes release starch as they are processed and the mixture can become gummy. Pour and scrape the brandade into a bowl. Process the remaining fish mixture, olive oil, and cream. Add salt, freshly ground black pepper, and Tabasco to taste. Serve on rounds of toasted bread.

NOTE: If you cannot find *herbes de Provence*, you can make your own by combining equal amounts of dried tarragon, rosemary, chervil, basil, and thyme.

Black Bean Dip

YIELD: about 2 cups

COOKING TIME: 12 to 18 hours for the frijoles negros

2 cups Frijoles Negros
(page 14), well drained

¼ cup bottled tomato salsa, or
more if desired, well drained

¼ to ½ teaspoon finely grated
lime zest

2 tablespoons strained fresh
lime juice

¼ cup plus 2 tablespoons
chopped fresh cilantro

Salt and freshly ground black
pepper

THIS IS A RECIPE IN WHICH HOME-COOKED beans have a far superior flavor to those from a can or jar. If you use vegetable broth, either store-bought, or made from the recipe on page 9, you will have a dip that vegetarians in your crowd can appreciate.

Place the beans, ¼ cup of the tomato salsa, ¼ teaspoon of the lime zest, the lime juice, and ¼ cup of the cilantro in the bowl of a food processor fitted with the metal blade. Process until it is a fairly smooth purée. Taste, and add salt and pepper and additional salsa and lime zest as desired. Garnish with the remaining 2 tablespoons of cilantro and serve with tortilla chips.

Duck Pâté

YIELD: about 2 cups

COOKING TIME: 6 to 8 hours for the duck

2 cups duck meat chunks from Braised Duck (page 129)

8 tablespoons (1 stick) unsalted butter, softened

2 teaspoons dried *herbes de Provence* (see Note)

3 to 4 tablespoons Cognac or reserved cooking stock from Braised Duck, optional

Salt and freshly ground black pepper

4 tablespoons (½ stick) unsalted butter, melted

Toast points or crackers

THE MAIN INGREDIENT FOR THIS QUICK, EASY, and wonderfully satisfying appetizer is the Braised Duck on page 129.

Place the duck meat in the work bowl of a food processor fitted with the metal blade. Pulse until the duck is coarsely ground. Add the softened butter and process until the mixture is smooth. Add the *herbes de Provence*, optional Cognac, and salt and pepper to taste (I like lots of pepper), and process until combined. Scrape the mixture into a ramekin and pour the melted butter on top. Refrigerate until ready to serve. Pass with toast points or crackers.

NOTE: If you cannot find *herbes de Provence*, you can make your own by combining equal amounts of dried tarragon, rosemary, chervil, basil, and thyme.

Caramelized Garlic

YIELD: 5 to 6 large cloves or 12 to 18 small cloves

COOKING TIME: 5 to 8 hours on HIGH

SLOW COOKER SIZE: 1 quart

1 bulb elephant or 2 bulbs regular garlic, intact

Olive or vegetable oil

Good quality, crusty bread, thickly sliced

EVERY TRENDY RESTAURANT, AT ONE TIME OR another, has set out roasted garlic along with slices of crusty bread on which to smear it. Using the oversized elephant garlic gives a milder flavor, but the regular variety is just as tasty if a little more pungent. If you are only cooking one bulb, it's best to use a small (1-quart) slow cooker.

To prepare the garlic, use a serrated knife to cut off one-fourth of the top of the bulb, exposing just the tops of the cloves. Place the garlic, cut side up, in the insert of the slow cooker. Pour in oil to come about one third of the way up the sides of the garlic bulb. Cover and cook on HIGH for 4 to 6 hours, or until the garlic is very soft when pierced with the point of a sharp knife. Cool the garlic bulb in the oil.

To serve, place the whole bulb in the center of a rimmed plate. Pour some of the garlic oil around it. Pass the bread. Squeeze the softened cloves of garlic onto the bread.

NOTE: The fragrant garlic oil can be stored in the refrigerator in a tightly covered container for 1 month. Use it in salad dressings, to baste broiled fish, and drizzle it over soup, pasta, or grilled vegetables.

Cipollinis and Baby Artichokes

YIELD: 6 appetizer servings or 4 servings as a pasta sauce

COOKING TIME: 6 to 7 hours on LOW or 3½ hours on HIGH

SLOW COOKER SIZE: 2½ or 3 quart

1½ pounds cipollinis, trimmed, peeled, and left whole (see Note)

3 garlic cloves, peeled and minced

1½ pounds baby artichokes (the very smallest you can find), stem ends trimmed and peeled, tiniest bottom leaves removed

2 teaspoons salt

½ cup olive oil

Freshly grated cheese, preferably Parmigiano-Reggiano

THIS IS A FIVE-STAR RECIPE THAT YOU CAN SERVE as part of an antipasto course or as an earthy pasta sauce for an elegant occasion. As the artichokes cook, they turn an amazing bronze color and fill the kitchen with a wonderful aroma. If you love the cipollini onions in this recipe, try the Cipollini Mashed Potatoes (page 70).

Place the onions in the bottom of the insert of the slow cooker. Sprinkle the garlic over the onions, and scatter the artichokes on top. Sprinkle with salt, and then drizzle the oil over the vegetables. Cover and cook on LOW for 6 to 7 hours or on HIGH for 3½ hours, until the vegetables are very tender.

To serve alone or as part of an antipasto platter, cool the vegetables to room temperature, drizzle with some of the flavored cooking oil, and sprinkle with cheese.

VARIATION: To serve as a pasta sauce, cook 1 pound ziti or other tube-shaped pasta in boiling water until al dente. Divide the pasta among 4 deep plates. Spoon the onions and some of the oil over the pasta. Place some of the artichokes around the rim of each plate and sprinkle generously with freshly grated cheese and black pepper.

NOTE: To peel small onions easily, plunge them into boiling water for 10 to 15 seconds. Transfer them with a slotted spoon to a bowl of cold water. The skins will slip right off when loosened with a small, sharp knife.

Fennel Agrodolce

YIELD: 4 servings

COOKING TIME: 1½ to 2 hours on HIGH

SLOW COOKER SIZE: 4 quart

2 medium fennel bulbs

2 tablespoons butter

3 shallots, peeled and finely chopped

⅓ cup golden raisins

2 tablespoons granulated sugar

⅓ cup balsamic vinegar

¾ teaspoon salt, plus more if needed

Freshly ground black pepper

1 teaspoon toasted fennel seeds, crushed (see Note)

THIS ITALIAN SWEET-AND-SOUR VEGETABLE STEW is good on its own or as part of an antipasto platter. Available year-round, fennel's licorice-like taste adds zesty flavor to this classic dish. If you've never cooked fennel before, taste before you cook. Served raw, it's a wonderful low-calorie snack.

Trim the rough bases and leafy stalks from the fennel bulbs. Chop ¼ cup of the leafy fronds and set aside. Discard the rest of the trimmings, and cut the bulbs lengthwise into ¼-inch-wide strips.

Melt the butter in a large sauté pan over medium heat. Cook the shallots until they begin to soften, and then add the fennel. Cook for 5 minutes, stirring to coat the fennel with the butter. Scrape the fennel and shallots into the insert of the slow cooker, then stir in the raisins.

In a spouted measuring cup combine the sugar, balsamic vinegar, and ¾ teaspoon salt. Stir well with a fork, and then pour over the fennel. Stir to combine well, cover, and cook on HIGH for 1½ to 2 hours, until the fennel is tender but not mushy.

Remove the fennel from the insert and transfer to a bowl to cool. Season generously with pepper, and sprinkle with chopped fennel fronds and crushed fennel seeds before serving.

NOTE: To toast and crush fennel seeds, place them in a small sauté pan over medium heat. Cook, stirring frequently, just until the seeds are fragrant and slightly browned. Remove them from the heat as soon as they start to brown, because they burn easily. Crush with a mortar and pestle, or place in a small resealable plastic bag and crush them with a rolling pin or meat pounder.

Roasted Vegetable Antipasto

YIELD: 6 appetizer servings

COOKING TIME: 8 to 9 hours on LOW or 3 to 4 hours on HIGH

SLOW COOKER SIZE: 5 to 6 quart

3 large carrots, peeled and cut into 3-inch strips, ½ inch wide and ¼ inch thick

2 parsnips, peeled and cut into 3-inch strips, ½ inch wide and ¼ inch thick

2 turnips, peeled and cut into 2-inch chunks

24 pearl or cipollini onions, peeled and left whole (see Note)

1 large red bell pepper, seeded and cut into 3-inch by 2-inch strips

1 large yellow bell pepper, seeded and cut into 3-inch by 2-inch strips

1 medium fennel bulb, rough base and leafy stalks discarded, bulb cut lengthwise into 3-inch-long slices, ½ inch thick

12 baby artichokes with stems intact, stems peeled

8 ounces large mushrooms, cleaned and cut into ¾-inch slices

YOU'RE CRAVING ROASTED VEGETABLES BUT don't want to turn on the oven. Making them in the slow cooker is the perfect solution.

Place the carrots, parsnips, turnips, onions, red and yellow peppers, fennel, artichokes, and mushrooms in the insert of the slow cooker. Sprinkle with the garlic, then toss to combine. Drizzle the oil over the vegetables and sprinkle with the salt and pepper to taste. Cover and cook for 8 to 9 hours on LOW or for 3 to 4 hours on HIGH, until the vegetables are tender but not completely limp.

If you want the vegetables browned, place them in a single layer on a heavy baking sheet, broil for 3 to 4 minutes, turn them, and broil another few minutes until browned.

Allow the vegetables to cool to room temperature. Arrange on a platter, drizzle with the cooking oil, and sprinkle with additional salt and pepper, if needed.

4 garlic cloves, peeled and minced

1 cup garlic-flavored oil from Caramelized Garlic (page 40), or mild olive oil, or a combination of the two oils

¾ teaspoon salt

Freshly ground black pepper

NOTE: To peel small onions easily, plunge them into boiling water for 10 to 15 seconds. Transfer them with a slotted spoon to a bowl of cold water. The skins will slip right off when loosened with a small, sharp knife.

Radicchio with Raisins and Brown Sugar

YIELD: 4 to 6 servings

COOKING TIME: 3 to 5 hours on HIGH

SLOW COOKER SIZE: for 1 head, use the 1-quart size;
for 2 to 4 heads, use a 3 quart or larger

2 heads radicchio, trimmed and cut lengthwise into 1-inch slices

4 tablespoons butter

¼ cup packed brown sugar

Finely grated zest of 1 lemon

3 tablespoons soy sauce

½ cup raisins

THIS ROBUST PREPARATION GIVES COLOR, TEXture, and flavor to an antipasto platter, or you can serve it as an alternative to coleslaw.

Place all the ingredients in the insert of the slow cooker. Stir to combine. Cover and cook on HIGH for 3 to 5 hours, or until the radicchio is wilted and quite soft. Serve hot or at room temperature as a side vegetable or as part of an antipasto platter.

Soups

Millie's Chicken Soup

YIELD: 6 to 8 servings

COOKING TIME: 5 hours on LOW or 3 hours on HIGH

SLOW COOKER SIZE: 5½ to 6 quart

1 (5- to 6-pound) fowl (an older roasting chicken, usually available in kosher meat markets), or 1 large roasting chicken, cut into pieces

2 large carrots, peeled and cut into 2-inch pieces

2 parsnips, peeled and cut into 2-inch pieces

1 large onion, peeled and thickly sliced

2 teaspoons dried dill weed

1 tablespoon kosher salt

2 teaspoons freshly ground black pepper

8 cups low-sodium chicken broth or Chicken Stock (page 8)

Fresh dill sprigs

MY MOM (THE FAMOUS MILLIE APTER, WHO wrote *Bread Machine Baking: Perfect Every Time* with me) has moved to an apartment with a tiny kitchen. She couldn't take most of her appliances, so she settled for her bread machine and slow cooker. On Fridays she uses the bread machine to make challah and the slow cooker to make her famous chicken soup. Since the machines do the bulk of the work, she has time for aerobics, yoga, golf, book groups, and movies. Starting with homemade or a good quality commercial chicken broth adds flavor and richness to this soup.

Place the chicken, carrots, parsnips, onion, dried dill, salt, and pepper in the insert of the slow cooker. Pour in the broth. Cover and cook on LOW for 5 hours or on HIGH for 3 hours, until the chicken is extremely tender and falls off the bone. Use a slotted spoon to remove the chicken and vegetables to a large bowl or platter. When the chicken is cool enough to handle, remove the meat from the bones, and set aside with the vegetables. Discard the bones and skin.

Strain the broth into a large bowl, then use a shallow metal spoon to skim the fat from the top. (Save it for Chopped Liver, page 31.) Taste, and add additional salt and pepper if needed.

To serve, spoon some chicken and vegetables into shallow soup plates, then ladle the broth over them. Sprinkle each serving with some fresh dill sprigs.

Double Celery Soup

YIELD: 6 servings

COOKING TIME: 4 to 4½ hours on HIGH

SLOW COOKER SIZE: 4 quart

8 celery stalks (with leafy tops if possible), trimmed and cut into ½-inch lengths (about 3 cups)

1 large celery root (about 1½ pounds), peeled and cut into 1-inch dice (about 4 cups)

1 medium onion, peeled and chopped

4 cups low-sodium chicken broth, vegetable broth, Chicken Stock (page 8), or Vegetable Stock (page 9), plus more if needed

¾ cup heavy cream

Salt and freshly ground black pepper

Finely chopped fresh chives

IF YOU'VE NEVER USED CELERY ROOT (CELERIAC) before, this is a good introduction. Don't be put off by celery root's appearance; beneath that scruffy exterior lies a flavorful root vegetable similar in taste to a turnip or parsnip. The easiest way to peel it is with a sharp paring knife. Shave off the outer covering until you reach the root's clean, white interior. I prefer this soup ice cold, but it can be served piping hot as well.

Place the celery (and leaves), celery root, onion, and broth or stock in the insert of the slow cooker. Cover, set on HIGH, and cook for 4 hours, or until the vegetables are very soft. Let the soup cool for 20 minutes, then purée it with an immersion blender right in the insert. (Alternatively, the soup can be puréed in batches in a food processor fitted with the metal blade or in a blender.) Stir in the cream and add salt and pepper to taste. Serve hot or chilled, garnished with chives.

Curried Cauliflower-Parsnip Bisque

YIELD: 8 servings

COOKING TIME: 6 to 7 hours on LOW or 4 hours on HIGH

SLOW COOKER SIZE: 5 quart

2 tablespoons butter or vegetable oil

1 large onion, peeled and thinly sliced

2 pounds parsnips, peeled and cut into 2-inch-thick slices

1 medium head cauliflower, stem and outer leaves removed, broken into florets

6 cups low-sodium chicken broth, vegetable broth, Chicken Stock (page 8) or Vegetable Stock (page 9)

1½ teaspoons curry powder

2 teaspoons salt

Freshly ground black pepper to taste

THIS LOVELY SOUP IS SWEETENED WITH PARSNIPS and thickened with puréed vegetables. Served hot, it will warm the frostiest winter evening; served cold, it will refresh you on a summer day.

Heat the butter or oil in a large sauté pan over medium heat and sauté the onion until it has softened. Scrape it into the insert of the slow cooker. (If your microwave oven is large enough to hold the slow cooker insert, place the butter and onion in the insert, cover with the inverted lid or a flat plate, place the insert in the microwave, and cook on HIGH for 4 to 5 minutes, or until the onion has softened.)

Place all the ingredients into the insert, cover, and cook on LOW for 6 to 7 hours, or on HIGH for 4 hours, until the vegetables are very soft.

Purée the soup with an immersion blender right in the insert. (Alternatively, the soup can be puréed in batches in a food processor fitted with the metal blade or in a blender.)

Taste and add additional salt and pepper as needed. Serve the soup hot or cold.

Tomato Florentine Soup

YIELD: 8 servings

COOKING TIME: 4 to 5 hours on HIGH

SLOW COOKER SIZE: 4 quart

2 large carrots, peeled and cut into ½-inch dice

3 celery stalks, cut into ½-inch dice

2 medium onions, peeled and diced

1 (10-ounce) bag triple-washed spinach, stemmed and torn into small pieces

1 garlic clove, peeled and minced

4 cups vegetable broth or Vegetable Stock (page 9)

1 (28-ounce) can crushed tomatoes in purée

1 cup apple juice

2 bay leaves

½ teaspoon Old Bay Seasoning

½ teaspoon Bell's Seasoning

Pinch of ground cloves

Salt and freshly ground black pepper

½ cup uncooked couscous

Freshly grated Parmesan cheese, preferably Parmigiano-Reggiano

TANGY AND ELEGANT, THE BRIGHT FLAVOR AND beautiful color of this soup make it a perfect first course. The addition of couscous thickens the soup slightly and gives it a pleasing texture.

Combine the carrots, celery, onions, spinach, garlic, broth, tomatoes, apple juice, bay leaves, Old Bay Seasoning, Bell's Seasoning, cloves, and salt and pepper to taste in the insert of the slow cooker. Cover and cook on HIGH for 4 hours, or until the vegetables are tender. Remove the bay leaves from the soup.

If you are going to serve the soup in 30 minutes, stir the couscous into the hot soup, and continue to cook, covered, on HIGH for 30 minutes. If you are planning on serving the soup later, do not add the couscous. Transfer the soup to a large saucepan, allow to cool, and then refrigerate. When ready to serve, bring the soup to a boil. Stir in the couscous, remove the saucepan from the heat, and allow to sit, covered, for 10 minutes.

Sprinkle each serving with a little freshly grated cheese.

Caramelized Onion Soup

YIELD: 6 servings

COOKING TIME: 10 to 15 minutes for the soup; 12 to 14 hours for the onions

3 to 4 cups Caramelized Onions (page 10), drained

Cooking liquid from Caramelized Onions, plus enough low-sodium chicken broth, beef broth, vegetable broth, Chicken Stock (page 8), or Vegetable Stock (page 9) to make 6 cups

Salt and freshly ground black pepper

6 thick slices French bread, toasted

1 generous cup grated Gruyère cheese

REAL FRENCH ONION SOUP JUST GOT A WHOLE lot easier to make, thanks to the slow cooker.

Preheat the broiler to HIGH with the rack in the upper third of the oven. Place 6 ovenproof bowls on a heavy-duty rimmed baking sheet.

Combine the onions, cooking liquid, and broth in a large pot. Set it over medium-high heat and bring the mixture to a simmer. Season with salt and pepper to taste.

Ladle the hot soup into the bowls, top each one with a slice of toast, and sprinkle generously with cheese. Set the baking sheet under the broiler and broil until the cheese melts and begins to bubble. Serve immediately.

Carrot-Ginger Soup

YIELD: 6 to 8 servings

COOKING TIME: 2 hours on HIGH

SLOW COOKER SIZE: 4 quart

1 (2-inch) piece of fresh ginger, peeled

4 large shallots, peeled and cut in half

Grated zest of 1 large orange

2 pounds carrots, peeled and cut into 1-inch pieces

3 large Idaho potatoes, peeled and cut into 1-inch cubes

6 cups low-sodium chicken broth, vegetable broth, Chicken Stock (page 8), or Vegetable Stock (page 9)

1 cup orange juice

5 to 10 drops Tabasco, or to taste

2 to 3 tablespoons soy sauce, or to taste

Plain yogurt or sour cream for garnish

HOT OR COLD, THIS SOUP IS A GREAT STARTER and can be a meal in itself. It's thickened with potatoes—not cream—but tastes self-indulgent just the same.

Place the ginger, shallots, and orange zest in the work bowl of a food processor fitted with the metal blade and process until fine, about 10 seconds. Transfer the mixture to the insert of the slow cooker. Add the carrots, potatoes, broth, and orange juice. Cover and cook on HIGH for 2 hours, or until the vegetables are very soft.

Use a hand-held immersion blender to purée the soup right in the insert. (Alternatively, the soup can be puréed in batches in a food processor fitted with the metal blade or in a blender.) Taste the soup, then season with the Tabasco and soy sauce. Serve the soup hot or cold, garnished with a dollop of plain yogurt or sour cream.

Hearty Mushroom Barley Soup

YIELD: 8 servings

COOKING TIME: 6 hours on LOW or 3 hours on HIGH

SLOW COOKER SIZE: 4 quart

2 tablespoons butter or vegetable oil

2 shallots, peeled and chopped

1 ounce dried mushrooms of your choice, rinsed to remove dirt

1½ pounds white mushrooms, cleaned and sliced

2 large carrots, peeled and cut into 1-inch lengths

1 cup (8 ounces) uncooked pearl barley, rinsed in cool water and drained

4 cups low-sodium chicken broth, vegetable broth, Chicken Stock (page 8), or Vegetable Stock (page 9), plus more if needed

1 bay leaf

1 teaspoon dried thyme

Salt and freshly ground black pepper to taste

ALL YOU WILL NEED IS A SALAD AND A LOAF OF French bread to make a meal when you serve this substantial soup, made from a combination of fresh and dried mushrooms. Be sure to buy pearl, not hulled, barley. (Hulled barley is used for baking.) This makes a very thick soup, so if you want it a little thinner you can add some additional hot broth when the soup is cooked.

Heat the butter or oil in a small sauté pan over medium heat and sauté the shallots until they have softened. Scrape them into the insert of the slow cooker. (If your microwave oven is large enough to hold the slow cooker insert, place the oil and shallots in the insert, cover with the inverted lid or a flat plate, place the insert in the microwave, and cook on HIGH for 4 to 5 minutes, or until the shallots have softened.)

Add the remaining ingredients to the insert. Stir, cover, and cook on LOW for 6 hours or on HIGH for 3 hours. Remove the bay leaf and add additional broth, if desired, for a thinner soup. Season with additional salt and black pepper.

Lima Bean Soup

YIELD: about 8 cups; 4 to 6 servings

COOKING TIME: 15 to 20 minutes for the soup; 7 hours for the lima beans

SLOW COOKER SIZE: 4 quart

FOR THE SOUP

1 recipe Lima Beans with *herbes de Provence* (page 78), cooked until very soft, with cooking liquid

Low-sodium chicken broth, vegetable broth, Chicken Stock (page 8), or Vegetable Stock (page 9), as needed

Salt and freshly ground black pepper

FOR THE OPTIONAL GARNISHES

Crisply cooked and crumbled bacon or pancetta

Extra-virgin olive oil, Rosemary-Infused Oil (page 16), garlic oil from Caramelized Garlic (page 40), or other flavored oil

EVEN THE MOST DIE-HARD LIMA BEAN HATER will enjoy this springtime soup. Don't divulge the source of the great taste and wonderful texture until he or she has finished the last drop—and maybe not even then.

To make a hearty, chunky soup, use a hand-held potato masher to mash the beans with their cooking juices into a coarse purée. Transfer to a large saucepan and heat, stirring, over medium heat, until it is very hot. Add enough heated broth to achieve the desired consistency. Ladle the soup into bowls, season to taste with salt and papper, and sprinkle each serving with some crumbled bacon or pancetta.

For a smoother and more velvety soup, purée the beans with their cooking liquid right in the insert of the slow cooker using a hand-held immersion blender. Transfer the purée to a large saucepan, add the broth, and heat as described above. (Alternatively, the soup can be puréed in batches in a food processor fitted with the metal blade or in a blender. As it is puréed, transfer it to the saucepan. A blender will produce the smoothest soup.) Ladle the soup into bowls and drizzle each serving with extra-virgin or flavored olive oil.

VARIATION: For a one-dish meal, make the chunky version of the soup. Slice 1 pound of smoked sausage (such as kielbasa) into ¼-inch-thick slices and cook them in a little oil in a sauté pan while the soup heats. Simmer the cooked sausage in the soup for 5 minutes, and then serve.

Best Pea Soup

YIELD: 10 to 12 servings

COOKING TIME: 10 to 14 hours on HIGH

SLOW COOKER SIZE: 4 quart

1 large onion, peeled and diced

4 large carrots, peeled and cut into 2-inch lengths

3 garlic cloves, peeled and minced

2½ pounds flanken, cut into 3 pieces

1 pound dried green split peas, rinsed, drained, and picked over to remove any bits of dirt and debris

2 teaspoons dried thyme

2 teaspoons dried tarragon

6 cups low-sodium beef broth, vegetable broth, or Vegetable Stock (page 9), plus more if needed

Salt and freshly ground black pepper to taste

THE NEXT TIME YOU ARE IN THE MARKET FOR A hearty soup, look no farther. This classic split pea soup is made with flanken, which comes from the chuck end of the short ribs. Look in kosher meat markets or ask a butcher for this special cut. If you can't find flanken, short ribs make a fine substitute. Chunks of smoked turkey tossed in halfway through the cooking time are also tasty.

Place all the ingredients in the insert of the slow cooker and stir. Cover and cook on HIGH for 10 to 14 hours, or until the meat is very tender and falls off the bone. Remove the meat and tear into bite-size pieces. Return it to the soup. Stir in additional broth if the soup seems too thick. Taste, and add salt and pepper if needed.

Cream of Zucchini Soup

YIELD: 6 servings

COOKING TIME: 4 to 5 hours on LOW or 2 hours on HIGH

SLOW COOKER SIZE: 6 quart

3 tablespoons butter

1 large sweet onion, peeled and chopped

2 garlic cloves, peeled and minced

1 pound tender young zucchini, cut into 1-inch slices

1 pound Idaho potatoes, peeled and cut into 1-inch slices

4 large fresh sage leaves, stemmed and chopped

4 cups vegetable broth or Vegetable Stock (page 9)

½ cup heavy cream

Salt and freshly ground black pepper

FRESH SAGE ADDS A LOVELY LILT TO THE FLAVOR, and the little bit of cream adds a silky, slightly sweet smoothness. Served hot or cold, this beautiful soup is ideal for those warm summer days.

Heat the butter in a medium-size sauté pan over medium heat and sauté the onion and garlic until softened. Scrape them into the insert of the slow cooker. (If your microwave oven is large enough to hold the slow cooker insert, place the butter, onion, and garlic in the insert, cover with the inverted lid or a flat plate, place the insert in the microwave, and cook on HIGH for 4 to 5 minutes, or until the vegetables have softened.)

Add the zucchini, potatoes, sage, and broth to the insert. Cover and cook on LOW for 4 to 5 hours or on HIGH for 2 hours, until the vegetables are fork-tender. Use a hand-held immersion blender to purée the soup right in the slow cooker insert. (Alternatively, the soup can be puréed in batches in a food processor fitted with the metal blade or in a blender.) Stir in the cream, and season to taste with salt and pepper.

Transfer the puréed soup to a large saucepan, or place the insert, covered with the inverted lid or a flat plate, in a microwave oven and heat, or transfer the soup to a metal bowl and refrigerate until cold. Serve hot or chilled.

Jewel Bisque

YIELD: 8 servings

COOKING TIME: 6 hours on LOW or 3 hours on HIGH

SLOW COOKER SIZE: 6 quart

3 tablespoons olive oil or vegetable oil

3 large shallots, peeled and minced

2 pounds butternut squash, peeled, seeded, and cut into 2-inch cubes

2 pounds Jewel or regular yams, peeled and cut into 2-inch cubes

1 medium celery root (about 1 pound), peeled and cut into 1-inch cubes

7 cups low-sodium chicken broth, vegetable broth, Chicken Stock (page 8), or Vegetable Stock (page 9)

1 teaspoon dried marjoram or 2 sprigs fresh marjoram

2 teaspoons dried thyme or 3 sprigs fresh thyme

3 to 4 drops Tabasco

Salt and freshly ground black pepper to taste

Plain yogurt or sour cream

THE NAME COMES FROM JEWEL YAMS, WHICH can be found in the grocery section of your health foods store and in many supermarkets. You can also use regular yams, which won't be as intensely red but will taste just as good.

Heat the oil in a small sauté pan over medium heat and sauté the shallots until they have softened. Scrape them into the insert of the slow cooker. (If your microwave oven is large enough to hold the slow cooker insert, place the oil and shallots in the insert, cover with the inverted lid or a flat plate, place the insert in the microwave, and cook on HIGH for 4 to 5 minutes, or until the shallots have softened.)

Add the squash, yams, celery root, broth, marjoram, thyme, Tabasco, and salt and pepper to taste to the insert. Cover and cook on LOW for 6 hours or on HIGH for 3 hours, until the vegetables are fork-tender. Remove the fresh herbs if you have used them.

If you want the bisque to have a chunky texture, use a hand-held potato masher to achieve the desired consistency. For a smoother bisque, use a hand-held immersion blender to purée the soup right in the insert. (Alternatively, the soup can be puréed in batches in a food processor fitted with the metal blade or in a blender.) Serve hot, topped with a dollop of plain yogurt or sour cream.

Black Bean Soup

YIELD: 8 servings

COOKING TIME: 15 minutes for the soup; 12 to 18 hours for the frijoles negros

SLOW COOKER SIZE: 4 quart

8 cups Frijoles Negros (page 14)

3 to 4 cups low-sodium chicken broth, vegetable broth, Chicken Stock (page 8), or Vegetable Stock (page 9)

Salt and freshly ground black pepper

Tabasco

¼ to ⅓ cup sherry, optional

Sour cream or plain yogurt

Fresh cilantro leaves

SHERRY IS THE HIDDEN INGREDIENT IN THIS classic soup made from humble ingredients. You can purée it until it is velvety smooth, or leave some of the beans whole for added texture.

Place the beans and their cooking liquid in a large saucepan, and then use an immersion blender to purée them until smooth. (Alternatively, purée the beans and their liquid in batches in a processor fitted with the metal blade or in a blender and transfer to the saucepan.)

Add enough broth to thin the mixture to the consistency of a thick soup. Heat over medium heat until it simmers. Adjust the seasoning, adding salt, pepper, and Tabasco as desired. If you are adding the sherry, stir it in just before serving. Ladle into heated bowls, and top with a generous dollop of sour cream or yogurt and a few cilantro leaves.

Chickpea Stew

2 teaspoons olive oil

2 garlic cloves, peeled and minced

4 cups warm Slow Cooked Chickpeas and their liquid (page 15)

Juice of 1 lemon, strained

Salt

Cayenne pepper

1 cup low-sodium chicken broth or Chicken Stock (page 8), plus more if needed

About 1 teaspoon paprika

1½ tablespoons chopped fresh parsley

1 tablespoon toasted sesame seeds (see Note)

2 tablespoons extra-virgin olive oil

ANOTHER MEAL-IN-A-BOWL, THIS WILL FILL YOU up, leaving just enough room for some salad and a really great dessert. This soup freezes beautifully, so make extra to have on hand for another time.

Heat the 2 teaspoons of olive oil in a small sauté pan over medium heat and cook the garlic until softened and fragrant. Scrape the garlic and oil into the work bowl of a food processor fitted with the metal blade.

Add the chickpeas, lemon juice, and salt and cayenne to taste. Purée the mixture, and add enough broth to make a very smooth and creamy soup. Taste, and add more salt, if needed.

Transfer the soup to a medium saucepan and place over medium heat. When the soup is hot, ladle it into large soup bowls. Sprinkle each serving with some of the paprika, parsley, and sesame seeds. Drizzle with a little extra-virgin olive oil.

NOTE: To toast sesame seeds, place them in a small sauté pan over medium heat. Cook, stirring frequently, just until the seeds are light golden brown and fragrant. Remove them from the heat immediately, because they burn easily.

Chorizo and Chickpea Soup

YIELD: 7 to 10 servings

COOKING TIME: 6 to 7 hours on HIGH

SLOW COOKER SIZE: 4 to 6 quart

1 pound dried chickpeas, rinsed, drained, and picked over to remove any bits of dirt and debris

4 garlic cloves, peeled and minced

3 parsnips, peeled and diced

3 carrots, peeled and diced

2 celery stalks, diced

2 onions, peeled and diced

1 pound chorizo, diced (see Note)

Salt and freshly ground black pepper

8 cups low-sodium chicken or beef broth, vegetable broth, Chicken Stock (page 8), Vegetable Stock (page 9), or water

1 (5-inch) sprig fresh rosemary

THIS HEARTY, COMFORTING SOUP IS PERFECT for Sunday night supper. All you need is a loaf of bread and a green salad.

Place the chickpeas, garlic, parsnips, carrots, celery, onions, sausage, and salt and pepper to taste in the insert of the slow cooker and stir to combine. Add the broth, place the rosemary sprig on top, and cover. Cook on HIGH for 6 to 7 hours, or until the chickpeas are tender. Discard the rosemary sprig.

Use a hand-held immersion blender to purée about half of the soup right in the insert. (Alternatively, the soup can be partially puréed in a food processor fitted with the metal blade or in a blender.) You do not have to remove the sausage to purée the soup using any method; it will become finely chopped and will enhance the texture of the soup.

NOTE: Chorizo is available mild or hot; use hot for this soup.

Congee

YIELD: 8 to 10 servings

COOKING TIME: at least 12 hours or as long as 18 hours on LOW

SLOW COOKER SIZE: 4 quart

1 cup arborio rice

10 to 12 cups low-sodium chicken broth or water, or Chicken Stock (page 8)

1 tablespoon salt, or more to taste

2 cups cooked, shredded chicken or Braised Duck (page 129)

2 to 3 tablespoons grated fresh gingerroot

½ cup fresh cilantro leaves

I SUPPOSE ONE MIGHT CALL THIS VERY SPECIAL dish the Chinese equivalent of chicken soup, but to millions of people eating breakfast in Beijing or Hong Kong, congee is, in fact, what Rice Krispies are to Americans. A thick, rice-based soup, congee is simmered for hours in special pots on street corners and in restaurants. When the rice is soft and mushy, a variety of "mix ins" are added, such as salted fish, bits of ham, cooked onions or chicken, gingerroot, and fresh cilantro. While you can use almost any rice to make congee, I found that arborio (used to make risotto) provides the creamiest texture. While most of the congee I had in China was made with water, I prefer the flavor of chicken broth. Here's my favorite version.

Place the rice, broth or water, and 1 tablespoon of salt in the insert of the slow cooker. Cover and cook on LOW until the mixture has a porridgelike consistency, from 12 to 18 hours, adding more liquid if necessary to create a thick, yet soupy mixture. Add additional salt to taste if needed. Just before serving, stir in the chicken and gingerroot. Spoon into bowls and garnish with cilantro.

Virtuous Lentil Soup

YIELD: 6 to 8 servings

COOKING TIME: 5 to 6 hours on HIGH

SLOW COOKER SIZE: 4 quart

2 medium onions, peeled and diced

2 celery stalks, chopped

4 carrots, peeled and diced

2 parsnips, peeled and diced

2 garlic cloves, peeled and minced

1½ cups brown lentils, rinsed, drained, and picked over to remove any bits of dirt and debris

1 teaspoon dried thyme

8 cups vegetable broth or Vegetable Stock (page 9), plus more if needed

Salt and freshly ground black pepper

VEGETARIANS AND FOLKS WATCHING THEIR FAT intake will love this soup.

Combine the onions, celery, carrots, parsnips, garlic, lentils, thyme, and 8 cups of broth in the insert of the slow cooker. Cover and cook on HIGH until the lentils are soft and the vegetables are tender, about 5 hours. Add salt and pepper to taste. Add additional heated broth if the soup is too thick.

Cream of Chestnut Soup

YIELD: 8 servings

COOKING TIME: 15 to 20 minutes for the soup; 15 minutes for the potatoes; 2½ to 5 hours for the chestnuts

SLOW COOKER SIZE: 4 quart

2 tablespoons butter

1 large onion, peeled and chopped

8 cups low-sodium chicken or vegetable broth, Chicken Stock (page 8), or Vegetable Stock (page 9), plus more if needed

4 cups shelled Braised Chestnuts (page 12), crumbled

8 ounces yellow fingerling potatoes, cooked in boiling water until tender, peeled, and halved

½ cup heavy cream, plus more if needed

½ teaspoon ground cloves

Salt and freshly ground black pepper

DIMINUTIVE SWEET YELLOW FINGERLING POTA-toes and just a little cream thicken this luxurious soup. A great starter for a fall menu, it goes especially well with a main course of fish or fowl.

Heat the butter in a large saucepan over medium-high heat and sauté the onion until soft and translucent. Add the broth, 3 cups of the chestnuts, and the potatoes. Bring to a simmer and cook for 10 minutes, or until heated through. Stir in the cream, cloves, and salt and pepper to taste.

Purée with an immersion blender right in the saucepan. (Alternatively, the soup can be puréed in batches in a food processor fitted with the metal blade or in a blender.) It may be necessary to add more broth or heavy cream to achieve the desired consistency. Serve hot or cold. Garnish each serving with a few of the remaining crumbled chestnuts.

Vegetables
and Sides

Ragoût of Leeks, Fennel, and Celery

Yield: 6 cups; serves 3 to 4 as a main course

Cooking time: 5 hours on HIGH or 6 to 8 hours on LOW

Slow cooker size: 4 quart

2 large fennel bulbs, rough bases and leafy stalks discarded, bulbs cut lengthwise into 1-inch-wide slices

3 large leeks, white parts only, cut lengthwise into eighths and rinsed well

4 large celery stalks, with leaves, chopped

4 tablespoons butter

1 cup low-sodium chicken broth, vegetable broth, Chicken Stock (page 8), or Vegetable Stock (page 9)

Salt and freshly ground black pepper

The word *RAGOÛT* comes from the French verb *ragoûter*, which means "to stimulate the appetite." This dish promises to do just that. While traditional ragoût is made with meat, this hearty vegetable stew has none. To make it completely vegetarian, use vegetable broth or stock and mild olive oil instead of butter.

Place the fennel, leeks, celery, butter, broth, and salt and pepper to taste in the insert of the slow cooker. Cover, and cook on HIGH for 5 hours, or 6 to 8 hours on LOW, or until the vegetables are golden brown and very soft. Serve as a main course.

Variations: To make a vegetable purée, drain off and reserve the cooking liquid. Use a hand-held immersion blender to purée the vegetables right in the insert. (Alternatively, the vegetables can be puréed in batches in a food processor fitted with the metal blade or in a blender.) Add cooking liquid as needed to produce a purée of the desired consistency.

Leek, Fennel, and Celery Bisque

Simply add enough chicken or vegetable stock to the puréed vegetables (see above) to produce a rich, creamy soup.

Braised Radicchio with Butter and Sage

YIELD: 4 to 6 servings

COOKING TIME: 3 to 5 hours on HIGH

SLOW COOKER SIZE: 3 quart

2 heads radicchio, trimmed and cut lengthwise into 1-inch ribbons

8 tablespoons (1 stick) butter

6 fresh sage leaves, each cut in 4 pieces

Salt and freshly ground black pepper to taste

BRAISING RADICCHIO MELLOWS ITS SLIGHTLY bitter taste. This makes a perfect accompaniment for fish or poultry entrees.

Place the radicchio, butter, sage, and salt and pepper to taste in the insert of the slow cooker. Stir to combine, and then cover and cook on HIGH for 3 to 5 hours, or until the radicchio is wilted and quite soft.

Glazed Carrots and Shallots

YIELD: 6 servings

COOKING TIME: 4 to 5 hours on LOW or 3 hours on HIGH

SLOW COOKER SIZE: 4 quart

2 pounds whole peeled baby carrots

6 tablespoons balsamic vinegar

1 tablespoon salt

¼ cup packed dark brown sugar

4 tablespoons butter

8 shallots, peeled; large shallots cut into quarters and small shallots cut in half

A VEGETABLE SIDE DISH DOESN'T GET MUCH EAS-ier than this. Balsamic vinegar provides a sweet glaze to caramelized carrots and shallots. You can find peeled fresh baby carrots in the vegetable aisle of the supermarket.

Place the carrots in the insert of the slow cooker.

Pour the balsamic vinegar into a small nonreactive saucepan. Cook over medium-high heat until reduced by half, about 5 minutes. Remove from the heat and stir in the salt and brown sugar. Set aside.

Melt the butter in a medium sauté pan over medium-high heat, and add the shallots. Sauté for 5 to 7 minutes, or until the shallots begin to soften and the edges start to brown. Scrape them into the insert with the carrots, making sure to include the butter and cooking juices.

Pour the balsamic mixture over the vegetables and stir well. Cover and cook on LOW for 4 to 5 hours or on HIGH for 3 hours, until the vegetables are tender when pierced with the tip of a sharp knife.

Stewed Mushrooms

YIELD: 4 servings

COOKING TIME: 2 hours on HIGH

SLOW COOKER SIZE: 4 quart

1 teaspoon butter

2 large Portobello mushrooms, cleaned and cut into ¼-inch slices

3½ ounces oyster mushrooms, cleaned and cut apart, if necessary

10 ounces cremini (baby bella) mushrooms, cleaned and halved

1 tablespoon dried marjoram

1 bay leaf

1 rounded tablespoon all-purpose flour

½ teaspoon salt, plus more if needed

⅛ teaspoon freshly ground black pepper

THIS RECIPE MAKES GREAT USE OF THE DAZzling variety of exotic mushrooms available in supermarkets today. You can serve these as a side dish or a light appetizer.

Use the butter to lightly coat the insert of the slow cooker. Add the portobello, oyster, and cremini mushrooms, the marjoram, bay leaf, flour, ½ teaspoon salt, and the black pepper. Stir well, cover, and cook on HIGH for 2 hours. Remove the bay leaf. The mushrooms will be very tender.

Cipollini Mashed Potatoes

YIELD: 6 to 8 servings

COOKING TIME: 12 to 14 hours on LOW;
15 minutes to boil potatoes on the stove top

SLOW COOKER SIZE: 2 to 3 quart

8 ounces cipollini onions, trimmed, peeled, and left whole (see Note)

3 cloves elephant garlic or 6 large cloves regular garlic, peeled

6 tablespoons butter

6 Idaho potatoes, peeled and cut into 1-inch cubes

Salt and freshly ground black pepper

TAKE ADVANTAGE OF THE SHORT CIPOLLINI onion season (mid to late fall) with this recipe. This fragrant onionlike vegetable, which is related to the hyacinth family, is now more widely available and can be found not only in specialty food stores but in many supermarkets as well.

Place the cipollini onions, garlic, and butter in the insert of the slow cooker. Cover and cook on LOW for 12 to 14 hours, until the vegetables are very soft and dark mahogany brown. Drain, reserving the cooking liquid. Set aside the onions and garlic.

Bring a large saucepan of water to a boil. Add the potatoes and cook at a gentle simmer until they are fork-tender. Drain and return them to the saucepan over low heat. Shake the saucepan over the heat to dry out the potatoes.

Off the heat, add the drained onions and garlic and some of the cooking liquid. Use a hand-held potato masher to mash the potatoes with the onions and garlic to the desired consistency. Season with salt and pepper to taste.

VARIATIONS: Seasoned with salt and pepper, the caramelized whole onions and garlic with some of their juices make a wonderful pasta sauce. The drained vegetables are perfect as a pizza topping, and the onion- and garlic-flavored butter that rises to the top of the cooking liquid can be chilled and spread on French or Italian bread or used to flavor cooked vegetables or enhance sauces. After spreading the bread with this butter, warm it in the oven or toast it under the broiler.

NOTE: To peel small onions easily, plunge them into boiling water for 10 to 15 seconds. Transfer them with a slotted spoon to a bowl of cold water. The skins will slip right off when loosened with a small, sharp knife.

Garlic Smashed Potatoes

YIELD: 8 servings

COOKING TIME: 4 to 8 hours on HIGH for the potatoes; 5 to 8 hours for the optional carmelized garlic

SLOW COOKER SIZE: 4 quart

5 large cloves Caramelized Garlic (page 40), or 4 large garlic cloves, peeled, minced, and sautéed in 3 tablespoons of olive oil until translucent

3 pounds fingerling potatoes, scrubbed and halved

1 large onion, peeled and minced

2 to 3 cups low-sodium chicken broth, vegetable broth, Chicken Stock (page 8), or Vegetable Stock (page 9), plus more, if needed, to completely cover the potatoes

1 stick butter, softened

½ cup heavy cream, optional

Salt and freshly ground black pepper

3 to 4 tablespoons garlic-flavored oil from Caramelized Garlic, optional

WHO DOESN'T LOVE GARLIC, BUTTER, AND potatoes? When I put these ingredients into the slow cooker, I knew it was going to be a winner. You can use freshly sautéed garlic or the Caramelized Garlic on page 40 and its fragrant oil, which adds lots of flavor. Leave the potatoes unpeeled for a rustic look. If you use fresh garlic, add it at the beginning of the cooking process along with the potatoes. If you use caramelized garlic, add it along with the butter just before mashing.

Place the fresh garlic, potatoes, and onion in the insert of the slow cooker. Pour in enough broth to cover the potatoes. (If they are not covered, they will darken as they cook.) Cover and cook on HIGH for 4 to 8 hours, or until the potatoes are very soft. Use a ladle to scoop out most of the cooking liquid, and reserve it if you are going to use it as a lower-calorie option to the heavy cream when mashing the potatoes.

Add the butter and caramelized garlic, if using, to the potatoes and use a hand-held potato masher or a wooden spoon to mash the potatoes. Don't make them completely smooth; they are supposed to be a little lumpy. As you mash the potatoes, add heavy cream, if desired, or some of the reserved cooking liquid, until the right consistency is achieved. Season with salt and pepper to taste, and serve hot. For extra garlic flavor, pass a little garlic-flavored oil to drizzle on each serving.

Tamarind Sweet Potatoes

YIELD: about 6 cups potatoes; 4 to 6 servings

COOKING TIME: 4½ to 5 hours on HIGH

SLOW COOKER SIZE: 4 quart

3 pounds sweet potatoes, peeled and cut into 1-inch cubes

1 (2- by 1-inch) piece fresh ginger, peeled and minced

1 large onion, peeled and diced

1 stalk lemongrass, outer leaves discarded, stalk cut in half lengthwise (see Note)

1 tablespoon toasted mild sesame oil (see Note)

1½ teaspoons tamarind paste (see Note)

¼ cup plum vinegar (see Note)

¼ cup soy sauce

2 cups orange juice

Finely grated zest of 1 large lemon

Salt and freshly ground black pepper to taste

I WANDERED INTO AN INDIAN GROCERY STORE IN my neighborhood and perused the shelves for an ingredient I hadn't tried before. Tamarind paste caught my eye. The pulp from this sweet-and-sour ingredient (classified as a fruit) is a great complement to sweet potatoes. Serve as is, purée it for a side vegetable, or thin it with chicken stock and serve as a soup.

Place all of the ingredients in the insert of the slow cooker. Cover and cook on HIGH for 4½ to 5 hours, or until the potatoes are extremely tender. Discard the lemongrass. Taste and season with additional salt and pepper, if desired.

Transfer the potatoes with a slotted spoon to a warm serving platter. Cover with foil to keep warm. Pour the cooking liquid into a sauté pan and reduce it by half over high heat. It will be syrupy. Pour the syrup over the potatoes and serve.

NOTE: Lemongrass, sesame oil, tamarind paste, and plum vinegar are available in the Asian and Indian food sections of many supermarkets, in Asian and Indian markets, and in gourmet stores.

Sweet Potato Purée or Soup

To make a sweet potato purée, drain and reserve the cooking liquid from the potatoes. Use a hand-held immersion blender to purée the potatoes right in the insert. (Alternatively, the potatoes can be puréed in a food processor fitted with the metal blade or in a blender.) Add a little cooking liquid, if necessary, to achieve the desired consistency.

To make a thick soup, thin the puréed potatoes with their cooking liquid and some chicken or vegetable broth until the desired consistency is achieved.

Ginger Sweet Potatoes

Place the sweet potatoes, orange juice, and soy sauce in the insert of the slow cooker and add 4 tablespoons (1/2 stick) butter, 1/2 cup sweet (cream) sherry or additional orange juice, and 1/2 cup packed brown sugar. Proceed as for Tamarind Sweet Potatoes. These can also be served with their own glaze or made into a purée or soup.

Millie's Tzimmes

YIELD: 12 to 16 servings

COOKING TIME: 10 to 11 hours on HIGH

SLOW COOKER SIZE: 5$\frac{1}{2}$ to 6 quart

3 large carrots, peeled and chopped

3 medium onions, peeled and chopped

2 pounds sweet potatoes, peeled and thinly sliced

2 pounds yams, peeled and thinly sliced

1 cup (4 ounces) dried apple rings, cut in quarters

1$\frac{1}{2}$ cups (8 ounces) pitted prunes

1 cup (4 ounces) dried pears, coarsely chopped

1 cup (4 ounces) dried apricots, cut in half if large

1 cup (4 ounces) dried sweet cherries

$\frac{3}{4}$ cup (3 ounces) dried sour cherries

1 cup packed dark brown sugar

2 teaspoons ground cinnamon

2 cups orange juice

2 cups white wine (sweet or dry)

"So, what's the big *TZIMMES*?" my mother asked as she spooned heaping servings of this savory mixture of vegetables and dried fruit (and sometimes stewed meat) and passed plate after plate down the Passover table. The big *tzimmes* ("big deal") was that my father loathed everything about carrots. My father aside, this is one terrific dish—and you don't have to wait for a holiday. Prepared without meat, it will even satisfy vegetarians. This dish serves a crowd, but it's easy to cut by one third or half to make less.

Place the carrots, onions, sweet potatoes, yams, dried apples, prunes, dried pears, dried apricots, and dried sweet and sour cherries in the insert of the slow cooker. Stir to mix. Sprinkle the brown sugar and cinnamon on top. Pour in the orange juice and wine and add enough water to cover. Cover and cook on HIGH for 10 to 11 hours, or until the vegetables are very soft. Serve hot or at room temperature.

Sweet and Sour Braised Cabbage

YIELD: 6 servings

COOKING TIME: 3 to 5 hours on HIGH

SLOW COOKER SIZE: 4 quart

3 cups cooking juices from New England Boiled Dinner (page 91), or low-sodium beef broth, vegetable broth, or Vegetable Stock (page 9)

1 large head purple cabbage, outer leaves discarded, cabbage quartered, cored, and cut crosswise into 1-inch-thick slices

1 large onion, minced

½ cup honey mustard

½ cup packed dark brown sugar

⅓ cup soy sauce

1 teaspoon ground ginger

½ teaspoon ground nutmeg

⅓ cup red wine vinegar

2 to 3 teaspoons caraway seeds

Salt and freshly ground black pepper to taste

USE THE COOKING LIQUID FROM THE NEW England Boiled Dinner (page 91), or canned beef or vegetable broth for this lovely side dish; it can also be served as an entrée.

Place all of the ingredients in the insert of the slow cooker. Stir well to combine. Cover and cook on HIGH for 3 to 5 hours, or until the cabbage is very tender.

Drain off the liquid and place it in a saucepan or sauté pan. Cook on high heat without stirring until the liquid is reduced by two thirds; it will be syrupy and slightly thick. Pour the liquid back over the cabbage, and then season to taste, adding a bit more salt or vinegar, if desired.

Braised Sauerkraut

YIELD: 6 to 8 servings

COOKING TIME: 9 to 10 hours on LOW

SLOW COOKER SIZE: 4 quart

4 pounds (8 cups) sauerkraut, drained, well rinsed, and squeezed dry

1 medium onion, peeled and cut into ¼-inch slices

1 medium carrot, peeled, cut lengthwise in half, then crosswise into thin semicircles

2 garlic cloves, peeled and crushed

1½ teaspoons caraway seeds

1½ teaspoons dried thyme

2 bay leaves

12 juniper berries or ¼ cup gin

Freshly ground black pepper to taste

8 ounces kielbasa, cut into ¼-inch-thick rounds

2 smoked pork hocks

2 cups dry white wine

4 cups low-sodium chicken broth or Chicken Stock (page 8)

SAUERKRAUT IS AN ACQUIRED TASTE. IT TAKES some practice and many trips to the ballpark, where hot dogs without it are considered naked. This recipe, developed by my recipe tester, Emmy Clausing, is so good that you can hold the hot dog.

At the grocery store, choose only the sauerkraut sold in a plastic bag, not in a can. Rinse it well so that it's less vinegary.

Place the drained sauerkraut in the insert of the slow cooker. Add the onion, carrot, garlic, caraway seeds, thyme, bay leaves, juniper berries or gin, and black pepper. Combine them thoroughly with a fork or with your hands. Scatter the kielbasa on top and bury the hocks in the sauerkraut. Pour in the wine and broth. Cover and cook on LOW for 9 hours, until the juices are bubbling and the sauerkraut has lost its crunch.

Remove the smoked hocks. If there is any meat on them, remove it and add it to the sauerkraut. Discard the bay leaves. Serve the Braised Sauerkraut as is with boiled potatoes, or use as a base for a flavorful Choucroute Garnie (page 119).

Lima Beans with Herbes de Provence

YIELD: 4 to 6 servings

COOKING TIME: 4 hours on HIGH or 6 to 8 hours on LOW

SLOW COOKER SIZE: 3 to 4 quart

2 cups dried lima beans, rinsed, drained, and picked over to remove any bits of dirt and debris

4 cups low-sodium chicken broth, vegetable broth, Chicken Stock (page 8), or Vegetable Stock (page 9)

1 very large or 2 medium-size sweet onions, such as Vidalia or Spanish onion, peeled and diced

6 garlic cloves, peeled and minced

4 teaspoons dried *herbes de Provence* (see Note)

1 teaspoon coarse or sea salt, or more to taste

1 teaspoon freshly ground black pepper

3 to 4 tablespoons garlic-flavored oil from Caramelized Garlic (page 40) or Rosemary-Infused Oil (page 16), optional

THE OFTEN MALIGNED, HUMBLE LIMA BEAN takes on a whole new personality when paired with garlic, sweet onions, and *herbes de Provence*. You can slightly undercook the beans and serve them whole, or cook them a bit longer and make a vegetable purée. Although I used giant dried lima beans for a dramatic presentation, any size will do for this recipe. For a vegetarian dish, use vegetable broth in place of chicken broth.

Place the dried lima beans, broth, onions, garlic, *herbes de Provence*, salt, and pepper in the insert of the slow cooker. Stir to mix, then cover and cook on HIGH for 4 hours or on LOW for 6 to 8 hours, or until the beans are just tender. Taste, and add salt and pepper as needed. Use a slotted spoon to transfer the beans to a serving bowl or platter. Reserve the cooking liquid to make Lima Bean Soup (page 55). Drizzle the beans with the garlic-flavored oil, if desired.

NOTE: If you cannot find *herbes de Provence*, you can make your own by combining equal amounts of dried tarragon, rosemary, chervil, basil, and thyme leaves.

Variation: To make a purée to be served as a side vegetable dish, cook the beans for at least 7 hours on HIGH, or until the beans are extremely soft. Drain off and reserve the cooking liquid. Purée the beans right in the insert with an immersion blender until they are very smooth, adding cooking liquid as needed. (Alternatively, the beans can be puréed in batches in a food processor fitted with the metal blade or in a blender.) Pass the garlic- or rosemary-flavored oil to drizzle over the purée.

Flageolets with Thyme and Garlic

YIELD: 8 servings

COOKING TIME: 6 to 7 hours on HIGH for the flageolets; 5 to 8 hours for the garlic

SLOW COOKER SIZE: 4 quart

3 cups (18 ounces) dried flageolet beans, rinsed, drained, and picked over to remove any bits of dirt and debris

Pulp from 1 bulb Caramelized Garlic (page 40)

¼ cup fresh thyme leaves

4 to 5 cups low-sodium chicken broth, vegetable broth, Chicken Stock (page 8), or Vegetable Stock (page 9)

Salt and freshly ground black pepper to taste

THESE GARLIC-PERFUMED, BUTTERY, TENDER French kidney beans are the perfect thing to serve with Braised Lamb Shanks with Garlic and Rosemary (page 105). Cook them until they are soft, but not so long that they turn mushy and lose their characteristic shape. You can substitute dried baby lima beans for the flageolets if you wish.

Place all of the ingredients in the insert of the slow cooker. Stir to combine, cover, and cook on HIGH for 6 hours, adding more broth if necessary, until the beans are tender but not mushy. Before serving, season with additional salt and pepper, if desired.

Cannellini Beans with Leeks, Spinach, and Marjoram

Yield: 8 servings

Cooking time: 7 to 8 hours on LOW or 4 hours on HIGH

Slow cooker size: 5½ to 6 quart

3 tablespoons olive oil

4 garlic cloves, peeled and minced

1 pound dried cannellini beans, rinsed, drained, and picked over to remove any bits of dirt and debris

4 large leeks, white parts only, cut In half lengthwise, well rinsed, then thinly sliced into semicircles

4 ounces young spinach leaves, stemmed, well rinsed, and drained

4 sprigs fresh marjoram

4 cups vegetable broth or Vegetable Stock (page 9)

Salt and freshly ground black pepper

SMALLER THAN LIMA BEANS AND LARGER THAN French flageolets, cannellini beans are part of the kidney bean family. When cooked until just tender, cannellini beans hold their shape and—good news—when overcooked still look and taste mighty appealing. This versatile side dish will make the vegetarian in your family happy. If you serve this or any bean dish with a loaf of whole grain bread you will be offering a combination that forms a complete protein.

Heat the oil in a small sauté pan over medium heat and sauté the garlic until softened. Scrape it into the insert of the slow cooker. (If your microwave oven is large enough to hold the slow cooker insert, place the oil and garlic in the insert, cover with the inverted lid or a flat plate, place the insert in the microwave, and cook on HIGH for 4 to 5 minutes, or until the garlic has softened.)

Place the beans in the insert, and then add the leeks, spinach, marjoram, broth, and salt and pepper to taste. Cover and cook on LOW for 7 to 8 hours or on HIGH for 4 hours, until the beans are tender. Season with additional salt and pepper if needed, and serve as a side dish or stew.

Curried Chickpea and Cauliflower Stew

Yield: 8 to 10 servings

Cooking time: 8 to 12 hours on HIGH

Slow cooker size: 6 quart

1 large onion, peeled and chopped

4 garlic cloves, peeled and minced

1 pound dried chickpeas, rinsed, drained, and picked over to remove any bits of dirt and debris

1 (2½-pound) piece of flanken

16 small, unpeeled new potatoes, scrubbed

6 cups low-sodium beef broth, vegetable broth, or Vegetable Stock (page 9)

½ cup mild curry paste (see Note)

⅓ cup tomato paste

1 head cauliflower, stem end and outer leaves removed, broken into florets

Salt and freshly ground black pepper

Cranberry-Mango Chutney (recipe follows)

THIS IS MY ADAPTATION OF A CLASSIC INDIAN dish made of chickpeas, potatoes, and cauliflower cooked slowly in a rich, mild curry sauce. While this version contains beef (flanken, the same cut used in Best Pea Soup, page 56), you can easily make a vegetarian version by omitting the meat and using vegetable broth or stock.

Place the onion, garlic, chickpeas, flanken, potatoes, and 4 cups of the broth in the insert of the slow cooker.

Place the curry paste and tomato paste in a medium bowl with the remaining 2 cups of broth. Whisk to blend the pastes with the broth, and then add it to the insert. Cover and cook on HIGH for 8 to 10 hours, or until the chickpeas, meat, and potatoes are very soft.

Add the cauliflower and cook on HIGH for 1 more hour, or until the florets are tender when pierced with a fork. Add salt and pepper to taste. Serve with jasmine rice cooked with saffron, and Cranberry-Mango Chutney.

NOTE: Mild curry paste is available in the imported foods section of your supermarket or in specialty stores that sell Indian ingredients. I recommend Instant India.

Cranberry-Mango Chutney

YIELD: 4 cups

COOKING TIME: 4 to 6 hours on HIGH

SLOW COOKER SIZE: 3 quart

1 navel orange

1 lime

1 large unripe mango, peeled and sliced

12 ounces fresh cranberries, or frozen cranberries, defrosted and drained

2 garlic cloves, peeled and minced

1 medium onion, peeled and finely diced

1 small green apple, cored and cut into 1-inch cubes

1 (1- by 3-inch) piece fresh ginger, peeled and minced

1 cup packed brown sugar

IF YOU ARE LOOKING FOR A SLIGHTLY LESS TRA-ditional condiment to serve with Thanksgiving turkey, or for something to spice up game, roast beef, or lamb, then look no further than this zesty mélange of tart cranberries, punctuated by brilliant shots of flavor from fresh ginger and mellow, rich mango.

Rinse the orange and lime in several changes of boiling water to remove the wax. Cut each in half, and then into very thin slices. Place the orange and lime slices, mango, cranberries, garlic, onion, apple, ginger, and brown sugar in the insert of the slow cooker. Cover and cook on HIGH for 4 to 6 hours, or until the cranberries have burst and all the ingredients are soft. Turn the slow cooker off, remove the cover, and let the chutney cool in the insert.

Store the cooled chutney in a tightly covered sterilized container in the refrigerator for up to 6 months. Serve chilled or at room temperature as a condiment for poultry or meat.

Refried Beans

YIELD: about 3 cups; 4 to 6 servings

COOKING TIME: about 25 minutes for the refried beans;
12 to 18 hours for the frijoles negros

¼ cup vegetable oil or bacon drippings

1 medium onion, peeled and finely chopped

1 jalapeño pepper, seeded and minced (see Note)

2 cups Frijoles Negros (page 14), plus some of the cooking liquid, as needed

1 teaspoon ground cumin

Salt

Tabasco

Grated Monterey Jack or Cheddar cheese

COOKED MASHED BLACK BEANS ARE THE TYPICAL side dish in most authentic Mexican and Tex-Mex dishes. You'll find this simple preparation much tastier than the canned variety.

Heat the oil or drippings in a large, heavy skillet over medium heat. Add the onion and cook, stirring occasionally, for 5 to 7 minutes, or until translucent. Add the jalapeño pepper and cook 1 minute more. Add the beans and ½ to ⅔ cup of the bean cooking liquid and cook, using a spoon to mash the beans as you stir them, to form a coarse purée the consistency of mashed potatoes. Continue cooking, adding more liquid if necessary to keep the beans from sticking, for 15 to 20 minutes, or until the mixture is heated through and forms a thick pancake. Stir in the cumin and season with salt and Tabasco to taste. Top with the grated cheese and serve immediately.

NOTE: When you seed the jalapeño, be sure to wear rubber gloves, as the seeds contain most of the oil, which is extremely potent.

Meat

Horseradish Pot Roast

YIELD: 6 to 8 servings

COOKING TIME: 9 to 10 hours on LOW or 5 to 6 hours on HIGH

SLOW COOKER SIZE: 4 to 6 quart

1 (3- to 4-pound) boneless chuck roast, trimmed of visible fat

1 (6½-ounce) jar prepared horseradish, well drained

5 medium carrots, peeled and diced

3 medium potatoes, peeled and diced

2 medium onions, peeled and diced

Salt and freshly ground black pepper to taste

1 cup apple juice

½ cup sour cream

WHEN I WAS LITTLE, MY MOTHER USED TO grate her own horseradish from the root. I remember her weeping eyes and running nose, and my puzzlement about why she'd endure such agony to prepare something that made her suffer so. The first time I tasted horseradish from a jar, I realized that I had been spoiled by the freshly grated kind, which had much more punch. But the store-bought variety of this powerful root livens up this pot roast and warms your insides without setting off a flood of tears.

Place the meat in the insert of the slow cooker. Rub the horseradish all over the roast, and then add the carrots, potatoes, onions, salt and pepper to taste, and apple juice to the insert. Cover and cook for 9 to 10 hours on LOW or 5 to 6 hours on HIGH until the meat and vegetables are tender. Cooking on LOW will produce the most tender meat. If possible, turn the meat over halfway through the cooking time.

Transfer the meat to a cutting board and cut it crosswise into ¼-inch-thick slices. Place them on a warm serving platter. Skim the fat from the cooking juices. In a small bowl, whisk the sour cream with 1 cup of the meat cooking juices, and nap the sliced meat with the sauce.

Brisket

YIELD: 8 servings

COOKING TIME: 8 hours on LOW or 5 to 6 hours on HIGH

SLOW COOKER SIZE: 5½- to 6-quart oval

4 Idaho potatoes, peeled and cut into ½-inch slices

2 tablespoons vegetable oil

1 (5- to 6-pound) first-cut or flat-cut brisket

2 large onions, peeled and cut into ¼-inch slices

4 garlic cloves, peeled and minced

1 (12-ounce) can beer

½ cup low-sodium beef broth

4 celery stalks, cut into ½-inch slices

½ cup tomato paste

1 (14½-ounce) can stewed tomatoes

2 bay leaves

½ cup packed dark brown sugar

⅓ cup Dijon mustard

½ cup red wine vinegar

¼ cup regular molasses

⅓ cup soy sauce

1 teaspoon paprika

Salt and freshly ground black pepper to taste

I THINK THE SLOW COOKER WAS INVENTED WITH brisket in mind. This sweet and savory version is perfection itself, melting in your mouth. It's very important to buy a "first-cut" or "flat-cut" brisket, which has far less fat than other cuts.

Lay the potatoes across the bottom of the insert of the slow cooker.

Heat 1 tablespoon of the oil in a large sauté pan over medium-high heat. Brown the brisket well on all sides. Place the browned meat in the slow cooker insert. Add more oil, if needed, and sauté the onions until soft, about 4 minutes. Add the garlic and cook 2 minutes more. Scrape the vegetables into the insert.

Pour the beer and broth into the sauté pan and bring to a boil, scraping up the meat bits in the pan with a wooden spoon. Pour over the meat. Add the celery, tomato paste, stewed tomatoes, bay leaves, brown sugar, mustard, vinegar, molasses, soy sauce, and paprika to the insert. Cover and cook for 8 hours on LOW or 5 to 6 hours on HIGH, or until the meat is fork-tender.

Remove the meat to a cutting board and slice it thinly against the grain. Skim any fat from the cooking liquid, discard the bay leaves, taste for seasoning, and add salt and pepper. Transfer the meat and potatoes to a serving platter or serve them on individual plates. Spoon the cooking liquid on top or on the side.

Braised Beef with Mushrooms and Barley

YIELD: 8 servings

COOKING TIME: 8 hours on LOW or 5 hours on HIGH

SLOW COOKER SIZE: 6 quart

1 (3-pound) boneless beef chuck roast

1 tablespoon vegetable oil

Salt and freshly ground black pepper

5 (3-inch-long) fresh rosemary sprigs

8 ounces cremini (baby bella) mushrooms, stemmed, cleaned, and sliced

1 large onion, peeled and chopped

2 bay leaves

10 large garlic cloves, peeled and left whole

1¼ cups low-sodium beef broth

½ cup medium pearl barley

2 cups fresh baby peas, or frozen baby peas, defrosted

⅓ cup sour cream

THIS IS ANOTHER TENDER, SUCCULENT DISH made even better in the slow cooker where less expensive cuts of meat are made fork-tender. Be sure to use pearl barley, and not hulled barley, which is used in baking.

In a large skillet, brown the roast in the oil on all sides over medium-high heat. Place the meat in the insert of the slow cooker and sprinkle with salt and pepper. Scatter the rosemary sprigs, mushrooms, onion, bay leaves, and garlic around the roast. Pour the broth around the meat. Cover and cook on LOW for 5 hours or on HIGH for 3 hours. Quickly add the barley to the liquid, cover, and continue to cook for 3 more hours on LOW or 2 more hours on HIGH, until the beef and the barley are tender. Remove the bay leaves.

Transfer the roast from the insert to a carving board, slice, and place the meat on a serving platter. Stir the peas and sour cream into the cooking liquid left in the insert. Stir well to combine, and then pour the sauce over the meat.

Beef Bourguignon

YIELD: 6 servings

COOKING TIME: 12 hours on LOW or 6 to 8 hours on HIGH

SLOW COOKER SIZE: 5½-quart oval

FOR THE MARINADE

1 large carrot, peeled and sliced

3 garlic cloves, crushed and peeled

4 cups dry red wine

2 bay leaves

3 sprigs fresh flat-leaf parsley

4 sprigs fresh thyme

3 pounds boneless chuck roast, cut into ¾-inch cubes

FOR THE STEW

4 to 6 tablespoons vegetable oil

4 ounces pancetta or thickly sliced bacon, cut into ½-inch cubes

8 ounces white mushrooms, cleaned and sliced

16 small white onions, trimmed and peeled and left whole (see Note)

3 tablespoons all-purpose flour

2 garlic cloves, peeled and minced

THIS IS NOT YOUR MOTHER'S BEEF STEW—unless your mother used a slow cooker and really good red wine. Browning the meat first is a crucial step that gives substantial taste to the finished dish.

To marinate the meat, place the carrot, garlic, wine, bay leaves, parsley, and thyme in a gallon-size resealable plastic bag or a large nonreactive bowl. Add the meat and seal the bag or cover the bowl with plastic wrap. Refrigerate for 6 to 12 hours.

To make the stew, drain the meat and vegetables in a strainer set over a large bowl. Set the vegetables from the marinade aside in a bowl, and reserve the strained wine. Heat 2 tablespoons of the oil in a large sauté pan over medium-high heat. Brown the pancetta or bacon lightly, and place it in the insert of the slow cooker. Add more oil to the sauté pan, if necessary, and brown the reserved vegetables from the marinade. Place them in the slow cooker.

Dry the meat well with paper towels. Add 2 more tablespoons of the oil to the sauté pan over medium-high heat and brown the meat; you may have to brown it in batches so as not to crowd the pan. Transfer the meat to the insert. Put the mushrooms, onions, flour, minced garlic, pepper, salt, reserved wine, broth, and the bouquet garni in the insert. Cover and cook on LOW for 12 hours or on HIGH for 6 to 8 hours, until the meat and vegetables are tender when pierced with the tip of a small knife.

1 teaspoon freshly ground black pepper

1½ teaspoons salt

Wine from the marinade

1 cup low-sodium beef broth

1 bouquet garni (2 bay leaves, 3 sprigs fresh flat-leaf parsley, and 4 sprigs fresh thyme, wrapped in cheesecloth and tied with a piece of twine)

NOTE: To peel small onions easily, plunge them into boiling water for 10 to 15 seconds. Transfer them with a slotted spoon to a bowl of cold water. The skins will slip off when loosened with a small, sharp knife.

New England
Boiled Dinner

YIELD: 6 servings

COOKING TIME: 12 to 16 hours on HIGH

SLOW COOKER SIZE: 6 quart

3 large Idaho potatoes, peeled and cut into large cubes

3 pounds first-cut or flat-cut corned beef

4 carrots, peeled and cut into 2-inch sections

1 small head green cabbage, outer leaves discarded, cored, and cut into 8 wedges

16 small white onions, peeled and left whole (see Note)

2 (14½-ounce) cans low-sodium beef broth

1 cup Guinness Stout or other dark beer, or 1 cup additional beef broth

3 tablespoons Dijon mustard

⅔ cup packed dark brown sugar

1 tablespoon dried dill weed

3 whole cloves and 6 peppercorns, tied in cheesecloth

IF YOU'VE NEVER EATEN THIS HEARTY DISH, trust me that it tastes a million times better than its name suggests, especially with Guinness Stout added to the cooking liquid. I like to make this in my large oval slow cooker and serve it right from the crock in large shallow soup bowls with freshly baked corn bread, followed by Indian Pudding (page 187) for dessert. It's especially important to buy a "first-cut" or "flat-cut" corned beef, since most of the fat will have been trimmed off by the butcher.

Place the potatoes in the insert of the slow cooker. Place the corned beef on the potatoes, then distribute the carrots, cabbage, and white onions around and on top of the meat.

Put the broth, beer, mustard, brown sugar, and dried dill weed in a medium mixing bowl and whisk together until the sugar dissolves. Pour the mixture into the slow cooker, and then tuck the cheesecloth bag among the vegetables. Cover and cook on HIGH for 12 to 16 hours, or until the meat is very tender.

Remove the cheesecloth bag and place the meat on a cutting board. Slice it across the grain into ½-inch slices. Use a shallow spoon to skim off any accumulated fat from the top of the cooking liquid. (Don't expect a lot since the meat should be well trimmed.) Return the meat to the slow cooker to keep warm until ready to serve.

NOTES: To peel small onions easily, plunge them into boiling water for 10 to 15 seconds. Transfer them with a slotted spoon to a bowl of cold water. The skins will slip right off when loosened with a small, sharp knife.

This recipe generates a lot of very flavorful broth. You may wish to reserve the leftovers to use when making the Sweet and Sour Braised Cabbage on page 76.

Corned Beef Hash

YIELD: 8 servings

COOKING TIME: 2 to 3 hours on HIGH

SLOW COOKER SIZE: 4 to 6 quart

1 tablespoon butter

1 medium onion, peeled and finely chopped

4 cups finely chopped cold cooked corned beef from New England Boiled Dinner (page 91)

4 cups, finely chopped peeled baked potatoes

Freshly ground black pepper

MY HUSBAND, DAVID, IS A CONNOISSEUR OF corned beef hash, and a bit of a snob about it, I might add. He gives his highest rating to this version and suggests serving it with a couple of fried eggs for a hearty breakfast.

Heat the butter in a small sauté pan over medium heat and sauté the onion until it has softened. Scrape it into the insert of the slow cooker. (If your microwave oven is large enough to hold the slow cooker insert, place the butter and onion in the insert, cover with the inverted lid or a flat plate, place the insert in the microwave, and cook on HIGH for 4 to 5 minutes, or until the onion has softened.)

Add the meat, potatoes, and pepper to taste to the insert and stir the ingredients together well. Cover and cook on HIGH for 2 to 3 hours, or until the hash is hot all the way through.

Asian Short Ribs

YIELD: 4 to 6 servings

COOKING TIME: 6 hours on LOW

SLOW COOKER SIZE: 4 quart

2 tablespoons vegetable oil

4 pounds meaty beef short ribs

1 medium onion, peeled and chopped

1 celery stalk, chopped

1 large carrot, peeled and chopped

2 tablespoons peeled and chopped fresh ginger

2 tablespoons Chinese fermented black beans, rinsed (see Note)

1 tablespoon ancho chile powder (see Note), or to taste

4 garlic cloves, crushed and peeled

¼ cup soy sauce

1 cup dry red wine

2 cups low-sodium beef broth

1 teaspoon dried thyme

1 bay leaf

1 whole star anise

¼ teaspoon freshly ground black pepper

THIS DISH WAS INSPIRED BY MING TSAI'S recipe in his cookbook *Blue Ginger*. The combination of spices and herbs is somewhat unexpected but works marvelously well. Be sure to take the time to skim the fat from the cooking liquid before you serve it.

Heat 1 tablespoon of oil in a large, heavy sauté pan over medium-high heat. Brown the meat in batches so that you don't crowd the pan. Turn the meat so that it browns well on all sides, 5 to 6 minutes for each batch. Transfer the meat to the insert of the slow cooker. Pour out the meat fat in the sauté pan, and then add the remaining tablespoon of oil.

Add the onion, celery, and carrot to the pan and cook, stirring, over medium-high heat until they have softened, about 5 minutes. Add the ginger, black beans, and ancho chile powder; cook, stirring, until fragrant, about 2 minutes. Add the garlic, soy sauce, red wine, broth, thyme, bay leaf, star anise, and black pepper. Bring to a boil over high heat and scrape the browned bits of meat clinging to the bottom and sides of the pan with a wooden spoon as the mixture boils. Pour the stock mixture over the meat. Cover and cook on LOW for 6 hours, or until the meat is very tender and almost falling off the bone. Remove the bay leaf.

To serve, transfer the short ribs to a serving platter. Skim the fat off the cooking juices (the meat will render a considerable amount of fat during cooking), and then use a hand-held immersion blender to roughly purée the vegetable solids and cooking juices into a chunky sauce. (Alternatively, the sauce may be puréed in a blender or food processor.)

NOTES: Chinese fermented black beans are small black soybeans preserved in salt; they are sometimes called "salted black beans" or "Chinese black beans." Pungent and very salty, they are found in Asian markets and other specialty food stores. If you can't find them, add 2 tablespoons additional soy sauce to the recipe.

Ancho chile powder is made by pulverizing dried ancho chiles, with no other ingredients added. The powder is deep reddish brown. You can adjust the heat of the finished dish by adding more or less of the powder.

Skirt Steak with Cipollini Onions

YIELD: 6 servings

COOKING TIME: 7 hours on LOW or 3½ hours on HIGH

SLOW COOKER SIZE: 6 quart

⅓ cup all-purpose flour

3 pounds skirt steak, each piece cut into thirds

3 to 4 tablespoons olive oil

2 cups low-sodium beef broth

1 cup dry red wine

¼ cup balsamic vinegar

1 tablespoon soy sauce

2 tablespoons tomato paste

1⅓ pounds cipollini onions, trimmed, peeled, and left whole (see Note)

2 tablespoons green peppercorns; if packed in brine, rinse well (see Note)

¾ cup firm spicy green olives, pitted and coarsely chopped (see Note)

THIS DISH IS ONE OF MY ALL-TIME FAVORITE things to make in a slow cooker. Skirt steak melts in your mouth prepared this way, and green peppercorns and piquant olives wake up even the most jaded palates. Cipollini onions, which can be found in the fall and winter months in Italian and specialty produce stores, are bulbs of the grape hyacinth plant and have an exquisite sweet-pungent taste that make seeking them out worthwhile. Pearl onions can be substituted if you wish.

Place the flour in a shallow bowl and coat the meat on all sides, knocking off any excess flour. Set aside.

Heat 3 tablespoons of the oil in a large sauté pan set over high heat. Brown the meat a few pieces at a time. Be careful not to crowd the pan or the meat will steam, not brown. Add more oil to the pan as necessary. Transfer the browned meat to the insert of the slow cooker. Add the broth and red wine to the sauté pan and bring to a boil over high heat, using a wooden spoon to scrape any browned bits of meat clinging to the pan. Cook until the liquids have reduced by half. Pour the broth and wine mixture over the meat in the insert, and then add the vinegar, soy sauce, tomato paste, onions, and peppercorns. Cover and cook on LOW for 7 hours or on HIGH for 3½ hours, until the meat is extremely tender when pieced with a fork. Add the olives, and cook for another 20 minutes. Serve with Cipollini Mashed Potatoes (page 70).

NOTES: To peel small onions easily, plunge them into boiling water for 10 to 15 seconds. Transfer them with a slotted spoon to a bowl of cold water. The skins will slip right off when loosened with a small, sharp knife.

Green peppercorns are available preserved in brine or freeze-dried. Brined peppercorns should be rinsed before using in cooking, and must be refrigerated after opening. They can be kept in the refrigerator for 1 month. Freeze-dried peppercorns can be added directly to the recipe. Kept in a cool, dark place they will last for up to 6 months.

Spicy green olives, marinated in a spicy herb dressing, can be found in many gourmet food stores.

Grilled Flank Steak with Tangy Pineapple Sauce

YIELD: 4 servings

COOKING TIME: about 12 minutes for the steak; 2 to 4 hours for the pineapple sauce

2 pounds flank steak

2 cups Tangy Pineapple Sauce (recipe follows)

THE PINEAPPLE MARINADE LENDS A LOVELY sweet-and-sour flavor and leaves a crisp, deep brown crust. Take care not to overcook this cut—it should be very pink in the center. Those who like their meat well done can select pieces from the ends, which are thinner and will cook faster.

Use a sharp knife to score the surface of both sides of the steak with crisscrossing lines about ¼ inch deep to prevent the meat from curling as it cooks. Place the meat in a heavy-duty resealable plastic bag, pour in the pineapple sauce, and seal the bag, squeezing out the air. Knead the meat in the bag to cover it with the sauce. Refrigerate for at least 3 hours, or as long as 24 hours.

Preheat an oven broiler to HIGH with the rack 5 to 6 inches from the heat source. Place the meat on a rack in a roasting pan and spoon some of the pineapple sauce over it. Broil for about 6 minutes, and then turn the meat over and spoon a little more of the sauce on top. Continue to broil for 5 to 6 minutes, or until the meat is medium-rare. (Alternatively, cook the meat on a charcoal grill. Preheat the grill until the coals are red-hot and covered with a light coating of white ash. Lay the meat on the grill, spoon some of the pineapple sauce over it, and grill for about 6 minutes on each side.)

Remove the cooked meat to a carving platter and let it rest for 5 minutes. Slice the meat on the diagonal against the grain into ½-inch slices. Serve with noodles or rice.

Tangy Pineapple Sauce

YIELD: about 5 cups

COOKING TIME: 2 to 4 hours on HIGH

SLOW COOKER SIZE: 1 quart

1 fresh, ripe pineapple
(about 3 pounds)

1 cinnamon stick

⅓ cup light or dark rum, or
orange juice

⅓ cup light packed brown sugar

1 medium onion, peeled and
diced

1 cup dried currants

4 garlic cloves, peeled and
minced

1 (4- by 1-inch) piece fresh
ginger, peeled and julienned

¼ cup soy sauce

½ cup balsamic vinegar

5 whole cloves secured in
cheesecloth, or 1 teaspoon
ground cloves

THIS SWEET-AND-SOUR, PINEAPPLE-BASED MÉLANGE can be used as a marinade, as a cooking and grilling sauce, and as a condiment for cold meats and poultry. If you don't want to wrestle the tough outer skin off the pineapple, buy fresh sliced pineapple, available at many supermarkets, fruit stands, and health food stores.

Cut off the pineapple top and bottom. Cut the pineapple into quarters, and remove the fruit from the rind with a small knife. Remove the core and any small brown "eyes" and bristles. Cut into 1-inch chunks.

Place the pineapple, cinnamon stick, rum, brown sugar, onion, currants, garlic, ginger, soy sauce, vinegar, and cloves in the insert of the slow cooker. Stir well, cover, and cook on HIGH for 2 to 4 hours, or until the ginger is soft and the flavors have melded. The pineapple won't soften very much as it cooks.

Turn off the slow cooker and let the sauce cool, uncovered, in the insert. Spoon into a sterilized container and refrigerate. The sauce will keep for up to 6 months.

Braised Beef Tongue

YIELD: 6 servings

COOKING TIME: $4\frac{1}{2}$ hours on HIGH, and 15 to 20 minutes to reduce sauce on stove top

SLOW COOKER SIZE: 4 quart

FOR THE TONGUE

1 ($2\frac{1}{2}$- to 3-pound) whole beef tongue, rinsed under cool water

6 cups low-sodium beef broth

1 medium onion, peeled and chopped

1 medium carrot, peeled and chopped

1 celery stalk, cut into $\frac{1}{2}$-inch pieces

3 garlic cloves, crushed and peeled

3 sprigs fresh thyme

4 sprigs fresh flat-leaf parsley

FOR THE SAUCE

2 teaspoons vegetable oil

1 large shallot, peeled and minced

Half a small carrot, peeled and cut into $\frac{1}{4}$-inch dice

$\frac{1}{2}$ cup tawny port

Salt and freshly ground black pepper

ANOTHER MASTERPIECE FROM EMMY. "DON'T knock beef tongue until you've tried it," she says. The soft texture of this sweet, flavorful meat is perfectly complemented by the port sauce. Ask your butcher for whole fresh tongue, not a smoked or pickled one.

Place the tongue in the insert of the slow cooker. Add the broth, onion, carrot, celery, garlic, thyme, and parsley. Cover and cook on HIGH for $4\frac{1}{2}$ hours, or until the tongue is tender when pierced with the tip of a sharp knife. Transfer the tongue to a platter to cool. Skim the fat from the cooking liquid and set aside.

While the tongue is cooking, prepare the sauce. Heat the oil in a large saucepan over medium heat and cook the shallot and carrot until they are softened, about 4 minutes. Pour in the port and simmer it until it has reduced to $\frac{1}{4}$ cup. Pour the skimmed tongue cooking liquid through a strainer set over the saucepan with the port mixture, and discard the vegetables and herbs in the strainer. Bring the mixture to a boil and reduce to 2 cups. Season with salt and freshly ground black pepper to taste.

When the tongue is cool enough to handle, use a small, sharp knife to slit the rough outer skin and peel it away. It should come off easily. Cut away any fatty sections and gristle at the base of the tongue. Slice across the grain into thin or thick pieces, as desired, and serve with the reduced sauce.

Osso Buco with Gremolata

YIELD: 4 servings

COOKING TIME: 8 to 10 hours on HIGH

SLOW COOKER SIZE: 5½-quart oval

FOR THE OSSO BUCO

4 veal shanks (2½ to 3 pounds total)

Salt and freshly ground black pepper

2 to 4 tablespoons olive oil

1 large carrot, peeled and diced

1 celery stalk, diced

1 medium onion, peeled and diced

2 garlic cloves, peeled and minced

1 cup low-sodium beef broth

½ cup canned plum tomatoes, drained and coarsely chopped

½ cup dry white wine

2 bay leaves

Finely grated zest of 1 large orange

¼ teaspoon dried oregano

¼ teaspoon dried sage

CLASSIC ITALIAN CUISINE — SLOW COOKER EASY! Veal shanks can be found in butcher shops and by special order in many supermarkets.

You're going to need the largest slow cooker to make this classic Italian meal — and some marrow spoons (iced tea spoons also work well) to scoop the cooked marrow out of the center of the bones. This dish pairs wonderfully with the Risotto with Parmesan (page 160) spiked with crushed saffron (see the last variation).

Season the veal shanks generously with salt and pepper. Heat 2 tablespoons of the olive oil in a large sauté pan over medium-high heat, and brown the shanks on all sides, 6 to 8 minutes. (Make sure that the cut ends get browned, too.) Transfer the shanks to a plate. Heat more oil in the sauté pan, if necessary, and cook the carrot, celery, onion, and garlic over medium-high heat until softened, about 4 minutes.

Scrape the vegetables into the insert of the slow cooker, and arrange the veal shanks over the vegetables. Add the broth to the sauté pan and bring to a boil, scraping up the meat bits in the pan with a wooden spoon. Add to the insert along with the tomatoes, wine, bay leaves, orange zest, oregano, and sage to the veal. Cover and cook on HIGH for 8 to 10 hours, or until the veal is tender when pierced with the tip of a sharp knife. Remove the bay leaves.

FOR THE GREMOLATA

½ cup pine nuts, toasted and coarsely chopped (see Note)

¼ cup finely chopped fresh flat-leaf parsley

1 tablespoon plus 1 teaspoon grated lemon zest

While the veal is cooking, prepare the gremolata. In a small bowl mix together all of the ingredients. Set aside.

To serve, place a veal shank on each of 4 dinner plates. Pour some of the sauce over each shank, and top each with a generous portion of gremolata.

NOTE: To toast pine nuts, place them in a small sauté pan over medium heat. Cook, stirring frequently, until they are light golden brown and fragrant. Remove them from the heat immediately because they burn easily.

Rolled Veal Breast Stuffed with Sweet Sausage and Spinach

YIELD: 6 servings

COOKING TIME: 6 to 8 hours on LOW

SLOW COOKER SIZE: 4 quart

FOR THE STUFFING

4 cups water

3 ounces fresh spinach, stemmed, well rinsed, and drained

1 teaspoon vegetable oil

¼ cup finely chopped onion

2 ounces sweet Italian sausage meat, removed from the casing

5 to 6 fresh mushrooms, finely chopped, or 2 tablespoons Duxelles (page 11)

½ cup cooked white rice

½ teaspoon dried thyme

¼ teaspoon salt

⅛ teaspoon freshly ground black pepper

FOR THE VEAL

1 (1¾- to 2-pound) piece of boneless veal from a 3½- to 4-pound bone-in piece of veal breast; save bones, if possible

MAKE DINNER FOR COMPANY WITHOUT KEEPING an eye on the oven. You'll need your butcher to prepare the veal, but it's straightforward from then on. While veal breast in the supermarket meat section doesn't look very promising, once the bones have been removed and the meat has been rolled to enclose a savory stuffing, the meat will be transformed. Ask the butcher to remove the bones, leaving the meat in one piece (there may be some meaty scraps, as well). Be sure to ask for the bones back, as they cook along with the rolled breast and create a wonderfully gelatinous stock.

Make the stuffing. Bring the water to a boil in a small saucepan. Drop in the spinach and return the water to a boil. Drain the spinach and refresh under cold water. Squeeze the spinach dry and roughly chop. Place it in a medium bowl. Heat the oil in a small sauté pan. Add the onion and cook until it has softened. Add the sausage meat and chopped mushrooms. Cook, stirring, until the meat has lost its pink color. Scrape the onion and sausage mixture into the bowl with the spinach. Add the rice, thyme, salt, and pepper and stir well. Set aside.

Place the boned meat on a work surface. If you have some boneless meat scraps, place them at the narrowest edge of the large piece of veal and pound them onto the edge. Pound all the meat,

Salt and freshly ground black
pepper

1 tablespoon vegetable oil, plus
more if needed

Half a medium carrot, peeled and
cut into ½-inch dice

Half a medium onion, peeled and
cut into ½-inch dice

Half a medium celery stalk, cut
into ½-inch dice

½ cup sweet Marsala

3 cups low-sodium chicken broth
or Chicken Stock (page 8)

8 ounces fresh mushrooms,
cut into ¼-inch slices

2 garlic cloves, crushed and
peeled

1 teaspoon dried thyme

¼ teaspoon salt

if necessary, so that it is a rough rectangle no thicker than ½ inch. Season the surface generously with salt and pepper.

Arrange the meat so that the narrowest edge is in front of you. Spread the stuffing to within 1 inch of the edges of the meat. Roll the meat up jelly-roll style into a compact cylinder. Use butcher's twine to tie the cylinder in three places, and then tie a fourth length of twine around the meat lengthwise.

Heat the 1 tablespoon of vegetable oil in a large, heavy sauté pan over moderate heat. Brown the meat slowly (brown the bones, too, if you have any) so that all the surfaces and the rolled ends of the meat are nicely caramelized. Place the meat in the insert of the slow cooker, and strew the bones around the meat. Add more oil to the sauté pan, if necessary, and brown the carrot, onion, and celery over medium-high heat until the vegetables are slightly colored. Pour in the Marsala and bring to a boil. Use a wooden spoon to scrape the bits of browned meat clinging to the pan, and cook until reduced by half. Add the broth, sliced mushrooms, garlic, thyme, and salt. Bring to a boil and pour over the meat. Cover the slow cooker and cook on LOW for 6 hours, or until the meat is tender when pierced with the tip of a small knife.

Before serving, strain the cooking liquid into a medium saucepan, skim any fat, bring the liquid to a boil, and cook until the liquid has reduced to 2½ cups. Taste and add more salt, if necessary. Place the roast on a serving platter, remove the strings, and slice the meat into rounds. Pour the sauce over the rounds and serve.

Braised Lamb Shanks with Garlic and Rosemary

YIELD 6 servings

COOKING TIME: 6 hours on HIGH plus another 6 hours on LOW

SLOW COOKER SIZE: 5 quart

½ cup dry red wine

2 heaping tablespoons Dijon mustard

2 teaspoons kosher or coarse sea salt

1 teaspoon freshly ground black pepper

5 to 6 pounds lamb shanks, not trimmed of fat

1 large, firm head garlic (about 15 cloves), separated into cloves, each crushed and peeled (see Note)

2 medium yellow onions, peeled and coarsely chopped

1 large carrot, peeled and cut in ¼-inch slices

Finely grated zest of 1 large lemon

2 heaping tablespoons coarsely chopped fresh rosemary leaves

THERE WILL BE NO LEFTOVERS. THIS RECIPE will make you fall in love with your slow cooker. Your house will be perfumed with the aromas of southern France. Enjoy!

In a small bowl mix the red wine, mustard, salt, and pepper and place in the insert of the slow cooker. Layer the shanks in the insert so they fit. Scatter the remaining ingredients around and on the shanks. Cover and cook on HIGH for 6 hours. Use tongs to reverse the position of the shanks, top to bottom. Reduce the setting to LOW and cook for an additional 6 hours.

Use a slotted spoon to transfer the shanks to a serving platter. Skim the fat from the cooking juices, taste, and add salt and pepper, if needed. Pour the juices over the shanks, and serve.

NOTE: For a less assertive garlic taste, use elephant garlic.

Lamb You Can Eat with a Spoon

YIELD: 8 servings

COOKING TIME: 10 to 12 hours on LOW

SLOW COOKER SIZE: 5½- to 6-quart oval

2 tablespoons olive oil

3 shallots, peeled and minced

3 medium carrots, peeled and chopped

3 tablespoons packed dark brown sugar

⅓ cup balsamic vinegar

1 cup low-sodium beef broth

1 cup dry red wine

¼ cup Dijon mustard

2 tablespoons soy sauce

1 (6-pound) shoulder of lamb, boned and rolled (4 to 5 pounds after boning)

10 garlic cloves, peeled and quartered lengthwise to form 40 slivers

1 tablespoon dried *herbes de Provence* (see Note)

Flageolets with Fresh Rosemary (recipe follows), optional

THE INSPIRATION FOR THIS RECIPE COMES WITH an amusing tale. I listen to WBUR, the public radio station in Boston, and one afternoon a panicked man called the *Here and Now* program. Scott Haas was about to make dinner for Ruth Reichl, the former *New York Times* restaurant critic, and had a mild case of "stage fright." The entree was going to be something called "Lamb You Can Eat with a Spoon," which sounded absolutely heavenly. Scott generously shared the recipe, which I have adapted to the slow cooker. The lamb is tender and sublime, especially when served with Flageolets with Fresh Rosemary (recipe follows).

Heat the oil in a small sauté pan over medium heat and sauté the shallots until softened. Scrape them into the insert of the slow cooker. (If your microwave oven is large enough to hold the slow cooker insert, place the oil and shallots in the insert, cover with the inverted lid or a flat plate, place the insert in the microwave, and cook on HIGH for 4 to 5 minutes, or until the shallots have softened.)

Strew the carrots in the insert with the shallots. In a medium mixing bowl whisk together the brown sugar, vinegar, broth, wine, mustard, and soy sauce, and then pour the mixture over the carrots.

Use a small sharp knife to make tiny slits all over the surface of the lamb. Insert a sliver of garlic into each one. Place the meat in the slow cooker and sprinkle with the *herbes de Provence*. Cover and cook on LOW for 10 to 12 hours, or until the meat is extremely tender. Transfer the meat to a cutting board and cut into 1-inch slices. Transfer the slices to a serving platter, cover, and refrigerate for 2 to 6 hours while you prepare the Flageolets with Fresh Rosemary. Use the vegetable solids and cooking liquid in the slow cooker to make them.

NOTE: If you cannot find *herbes de Provence*, you can make your own by combining equal amounts of dried tarragon, rosemary, chervil, basil, and thyme.

Flageolets with Fresh Rosemary

YIELD: 6 servings

COOKING TIME: 5 to 6 hours on LOW or 2 to 3 hours on HIGH

Cooking juices and solids from Lamb You Can Eat With a Spoon

12 ounces dried flageolet beans, rinsed, drained, and picked over to remove any bits of dirt and debris

2 heaping tablespoons fresh rosemary leaves, chopped

To the lamb cooking juices in the slow cooker insert, add the beans, rosemary, salt, and pepper. Add beef broth, if necessary, so that the liquid covers the beans. Cover and cook on LOW for 5 to 6 hours, or on HIGH for 2 to 3 hours, until the beans are tender but have not lost their shape. Taste and season with salt and pepper.

2 teaspoons salt

1 teaspoon freshly ground black pepper

Low-sodium beef broth, if necessary

When ready to serve, reheat the lamb; a microwave works well for this, but make sure your platter is microwave-safe. (Alternatively, place the lamb on an ovenproof platter, cover with aluminum foil, and place in a preheated 250°F oven for 30 minutes.) For each serving, spoon some beans and their cooking liquid onto a dinner plate and top with slices of lamb.

Lamb Stew with Mashed Potato and Feta Crust

YIELD: 4 to 6 servings

COOKING TIME: 6 to 7 hours on LOW

SLOW COOKER SIZE: 4 to 6 quart

1 tablespoon olive oil, plus more if needed

3 pounds lamb stew meat, trimmed of fat, in 1-inch cubes

5 shallots, peeled and coarsely chopped

2 garlic cloves, peeled and coarsely chopped

1 cup dry red wine

1 cup low-sodium beef broth

⅛ teaspoon fennel seeds, crushed (see Note)

2 tablespoons chopped fresh dill

1 fennel bulb, rough base and leafy stalks discarded, bulb chopped into ½-inch dice

⅓ cup oil-cured black olives, pitted (see Note)

3 yellow-fleshed potatoes, such as Yukon Gold

¼ cup crumbled feta cheese

THIS ADAPTATION OF SHEPHERD'S PIE HAS A secret ingredient in the crust.

Heat 1 tablespoon of the olive oil in a large sauté pan over moderate heat. Brown the meat in batches, adding more oil if necessary. Do not crowd the meat in the pan or it will steam rather than brown. Transfer the meat to the insert of the slow cooker.

Add the shallots and garlic to the pan, cook until soft, and then scrape them into the insert. Pour the red wine and beef broth into the sauté pan. Bring it to a boil over high heat, using a wooden spoon to scrape up any browned bits of meat clinging to the pan. Reduce the liquid by half, then pour into the insert.

Add the fennel seeds, 1 tablespoon of the fresh dill, the fennel bulb, and olives. Stir to combine the ingredients, and then cover and cook on LOW for 6 to 7 hours, until the meat and fennel are tender when pierced with the tip of a sharp knife.

Meanwhile, peel and cube the potatoes. Cook them in a large pot of boiling water until they are tender, then drain them well. Return them to the pan and use a hand-held potato masher to mash them with the remaining 1 tablespoon of chopped dill and the feta cheese.

Preheat the broiler with a rack positioned so that the top of the slow cooker insert will be 4 to 5 inches from the heat source. Remove the slow cooker insert to a protected work surface.

Spread the potato mixture over the surface of the stew. Carefully place the insert under the preheated broiler and broil until the potato topping has browned. Be careful when you handle the insert because it will be very hot. Use a serving spoon to scoop up some filling and potato crust onto warm plates.

NOTES: Crush fennel seeds with a mortar and pestle or place in a small resealable plastic bag and crush with a rolling pin or meat pounder.

A cherry pitter is a handy tool for pitting olives. It won't work on the smallest ones, but most olives can be successfully pitted this way. Look for this hand-held tool in a kitchen supply store.

Lamb-Stuffed Cabbage Rolls
with Yogurt-Dill Sauce

YIELD: 4 servings

COOKING TIME: 8 hours on LOW or 4 hours on HIGH

SLOW COOKER SIZE: 2 to 3 quart

1 large head green cabbage (about 3 pounds), cored from the bottom and left whole

2 tablespoons olive oil

3 scallions, white parts only, thinly sliced

2 large garlic cloves, peeled and minced

1 pound lean ground lamb

2 cups plain yogurt

4 tablespoons chopped fresh dill

1 teaspoon Tabasco

1½ teaspoons salt

1 cup low-sodium chicken or beef broth, or Chicken Stock (page 8)

1 (14½-ounce) can stewed tomatoes

YOU CAN SERVE THESE AS A MAIN COURSE, A first course, or as a passed appetizer. Instead of boiling the cabbage to soften the leaves, try placing the head in the freezer for a couple of hours. After you have taken it out and defrosted it, the leaves will be pliable enough for wrapping, and your kitchen won't smell like cooked cabbage.

Freeze the cabbage for 2 hours and then defrost it. Alternatively, bring a large pot of water to a rapid boil. Add the cabbage, cored end down, and reduce the heat to medium. Cover and simmer until the leaves have softened, 10 to 12 minutes. Refresh the cabbage in a bowl of cold water.

When the cabbage has defrosted or is cool enough to handle, separate 16 large leaves from the head. Use a small sharp knife to cut out the thick section on the bottom of the leaves to allow the leaves to roll up easily. Set the leaves aside. Chop enough of the remaining cabbage leaves to make 3 cups.

Heat the oil in a large sauté pan over medium-high heat. Sauté the chopped cabbage, scallions, and garlic until tender, about 10 minutes, stirring occasionally. Use a slotted spoon to transfer the vegetables to a bowl. Increase the heat to high and sauté the lamb until well browned on all sides. Stir frequently and break up the lamb as it cooks. Add to the cabbage mixture.

In a food processor fitted with the steel blade, process the lamb and cabbage mixture until finely ground, but not mushy. Add ½ cup of yogurt, 2 tablespoons of the dill, the Tabasco, and salt, and pulse 2 or 3 times just to combine.

Flatten 1 reserved cabbage leaf on a work surface and place 3 tablespoons of the lamb mixture at the bottom of the leaf. Roll it up tightly to form a 3-inch-long roll, tucking in the ends as you go. Repeat with the remaining leaves and lamb mixture. Stack the rolls in as many layers as necessary to fit. Pour in the broth and tomatoes with their liquid. Cover and cook on LOW for 8 hours or on HIGH for 4 hours.

Just before serving, whisk together the remaining 1½ cups of yogurt and the remaining 2 tablespoons of dill. Set the sauce aside. When the rolls are done, transfer them to a platter and keep them warm. Pour the pan juices into a saucepan. Reduce the liquid by one third over high heat, and then pour the juices over the rolls and serve. Pass the yogurt-dill sauce separately.

Venison Stew
with Mushrooms

YIELD: 6 servings

COOKING TIME: 6 to 8 hours on LOW

SLOW COOKER SIZE: 4 quart

FOR THE MARINADE

¼ cup vegetable oil

¼ cup balsamic vinegar

¼ cup dry red wine

1 large sprig fresh rosemary

1 large sprig fresh thyme

1 tablespoon honey

2 tablespoons soy sauce

FOR THE STEW

2 pounds venison stew meat, cut into 1½-inch cubes

2 tablespoons vegetable oil, plus more if needed

1 large carrot, peeled and cut into ½-inch dice

1 medium onion, peeled and finely chopped

2 garlic cloves, crushed and peeled

1 tablespoon all-purpose flour

1½ cups dry red wine

THIS IS AN ADAPTATION OF A RECIPE IN *ALSACE Gastronomique* by Sue Style (Abbeville Press, 1996). I prefer making this dish in a slow cooker better than baking it as a traditional oven casserole because the venison is more tender and the flavor more intact. The meat marinates in a Provençal-inspired mixture overnight.

Combine the marinade ingredients in a large nonreactive mixing bowl or in a gallon-size resealable plastic bag. Place the meat in the bowl or bag. If you are using a bowl, stir the meat with the marinade ingredients, cover the bowl with plastic wrap, and refrigerate. If you are using a bag, seal it and knead the bag gently to distribute the marinade ingredients over the meat, and then refrigerate the bag. Allow the meat to marinate for 12 to 24 hours. Stir the meat in the bowl or squeeze the bag occasionally during the marination time.

When you are ready to cook the stew, drain the meat and discard the marinade. Dry the meat with paper towels. Heat the oil in a large, heavy-duty sauté pan over medium-high heat. Brown the meat without crowding the pan, turning it to brown on all sides. You may have to do this in several batches. Transfer the browned meat to the insert of the slow cooker. Add the carrot, onion, and garlic to the sauté pan and cook over medium heat for about 7 minutes, until the vegetables have softened. Sprinkle with the flour and cook, stirring, for about 2 minutes, until you can no longer see any white flour. Add the wine, broth, tomatoes, bay

1½ cups low-sodium beef broth

2 plum tomatoes, peeled, seeded, and chopped (see Note)

2 bay leaves

2 whole cloves

¾ teaspoon salt, plus more if needed

Freshly ground black pepper to taste

1 tablespoon butter

10 ounces cremini (baby bella) or other fresh mushrooms, cleaned and cut into ¼-inch slices

1 tablespoon red currant jelly

2 tablespoons chopped fresh flat-leaf parsley

leaves, cloves, ½ teaspoon of the salt, and pepper to taste to the pan. Bring the mixture to a boil over high heat, scraping up the browned bits of meat from the bottom of the pan. Pour the contents of the pan over the meat.

Cover and cook on LOW for 6 hours, or until the meat is tender when pierced with the tip of a sharp knife. Turn the slow cooker off and let the stew rest, covered, while you prepare the mushrooms.

Melt the butter in a large sauté pan over medium-high heat. Add the mushrooms and cook, stirring frequently, for about 10 minutes, until they have softened and browned. Sprinkle them with the remaining ¼ teaspoon salt. Set the mushrooms aside.

Ladle off about ½ cup of the cooking liquid from the stew and place it in a small saucepan. Bring it to a simmer, and then whisk in the currant jelly and continue whisking until it has dissolved. Pour the sweetened liquid back into the stew, stir well, and add the mushrooms. Season with additional salt, if needed, and pepper to taste. Remove the bay leaves. To serve, ladle the stew into wide, shallow bowls. Sprinkle with parsley.

NOTES: To peel tomatoes, plunge them into rapidly boiling water for 10 to 20 seconds, and then remove them with a slotted spoon. The skins will slip right off.

Since venison is hard to obtain, buy a double quantity in season. Double the marinade recipe; freeze half the meat in its marinade in a large, heavy-duty resealable plastic bag. It will keep for 6 months.

Braised Rabbit with Mustard Cream Sauce

YIELD: 4 servings

COOKING TIME: 7 hours on LOW or 3½ hours on HIGH

SLOW COOKER SIZE: 4 quart

3 slices (2½ ounces) bacon, cut into ½-inch squares

¼ cup all-purpose flour

1 tablespoon dry mustard

¼ teaspoon salt

¼ teaspoon freshly ground black pepper

1 (2¼- to 3-pound) "fryer" rabbit, cut into 8 pieces, rinsed, and patted dry

2 tablespoons vegetable oil

1 large onion, peeled and thinly sliced

⅓ cup dry white wine

3 cups low-sodium chicken broth, or Chicken Stock (page 8)

1 teaspoon dried thyme

1 bay leaf

2 garlic cloves, crushed and peeled

3 sprigs fresh flat-leaf parsley, plus 1 tablespoon chopped

¼ cup heavy cream

RAISING IS THE PERFECT COOKING METHOD FOR rabbit in this French-inspired dish. Most butchers can get fresh rabbit, or you can find it in the frozen meat section of many supermarkets and specialty food stores.

Heat a large sauté pan over medium-high heat and cook the bacon until crisp. Drain on paper towels, and leave the fat in the pan.

On a piece of waxed paper toss together the flour, dry mustard, salt, and pepper. Dredge the rabbit pieces in the seasoned flour. Add 1 tablespoon of the oil to the pan in which the bacon cooked. Heat over medium-high heat, and add the rabbit pieces. Brown the pieces well on all sides, and then remove to the insert of the slow cooker.

Add the remaining tablespoon of oil to the sauté pan and cook the onion over medium heat until it has softened. Pour in the wine and bring to a boil, scraping up any browned bits of meat clinging to the pan with a wooden spoon. Add the broth, thyme, bay leaf, garlic, and parsley sprigs. Bring to a boil and pour it over the rabbit. Crumble the bacon slices and add half of the bits to the insert. Cover and cook on LOW for 7 hours or on HIGH for 3½ hours, until the rabbit is tender when pierced with the tip of a sharp knife.

Strain the cooking liquid into a medium saucepan and reduce over high heat to 1½ cups. Taste and adjust the seasonings. In a

1 tablespoon Dijon mustard

2 teaspoons fresh thyme leaves

small bowl whisk together the heavy cream and Dijon mustard, and then stir the mixture into the sauce.

Place the rabbit pieces on a serving platter and pour the sauce over them. Sprinkle with the remaining bacon bits and the fresh thyme leaves and chopped parsley. Serve with buttered broad noodles or steamed yellow-fleshed potatoes.

Braised Pork Loin
with Port and Prunes

YIELD: 8 servings

COOKING TIME: 5 to 8 hours on HIGH

SLOW COOKER SIZE: 5½-quart oval

1½ teaspoons freshly ground black pepper

1 teaspoon salt

1 teaspoon dried sage

1 teaspoon dry mustard

½ teaspoon dried thyme

1 (4-pound) boneless pork loin roast

1 tablespoon olive oil

2 medium onions, peeled and sliced

1 large leek, white part only, rinsed well and finely chopped

1 large carrot, peeled and finely chopped

1 cup port

¾ cup low-sodium chicken broth or Chicken Stock (page 8)

1½ cups (10 ounces) pitted prunes

2 bay leaves

A SPRINKLING OF HERBS, A DASH OF MUSTARD, dried fruit, and a splash of red wine give this pork roast a complex multilayered taste.

In a small bowl combine the pepper, salt, sage, mustard, and thyme. Trim the excess fat from the pork and rub the surface of the roast with the spice mixture. Tie the roast at 2-inch intervals with heavy kitchen string.

Heat the olive oil in a large sauté pan over medium heat. Brown the pork on all sides and transfer to a plate. Add the onions, leek, and carrot to the pan. Cook for 5 minutes, stirring frequently. Scrape the vegetables into the insert of the slow cooker. Place the roast on top of the vegetables. Add the port, broth, prunes, and bay leaves. Cover and cook on HIGH for 5 to 8 hours, or until an instant-read thermometer inserted in the center registers 170°F. Remove the bay leaves. Transfer the roast to a carving board and slice. Place the sliced pork on a serving platter and keep it warm while you prepare the sauce.

Scoop 8 to 10 prunes and some of the cooking liquid from the insert into a food processor or blender; process until smooth. Return the puréed prunes to the remaining cooking liquid. Season with additional salt and pepper to taste. Pour the sauce over the pork before serving or pass it separately.

Honey-Glazed Spareribs

YIELD: 6 to 8 servings

COOKING TIME: 7 to 8 hours on LOW

SLOW COOKER SIZE: 6 quart

1 cup packed light brown sugar

1½ cups honey

¼ cup cider vinegar

¼ cup Worcestershire sauce

4 garlic cloves, crushed and peeled

1 tablespoon salt

2 teaspoons ground ginger

2 teaspoons Tabasco

6 pounds spareribs

JUST LIKE POTATO CHIPS, WE COULDN'T EAT JUST one. Gnaw these sweet-and-sour ribs right on the bone, or use a fork. The meat is so tender you won't need a knife.

In a medium, nonreactive saucepan slowly heat the brown sugar, honey, vinegar, and Worcestershire sauce until the sugar is completely dissolved. Remove the pan from the heat and add the garlic, salt, ginger, and Tabasco. Stir until completely combined. Let cool to room temperature.

Divide the spareribs between 2 jumbo (2-gallon) heavy-duty resealable plastic bags. Pour half the marinade into each bag, press out the air, and seal the bags.

Place the bags in a large roasting pan, and refrigerate for 12 to 24 hours. Turn over the bags 2 or 3 times during marination so that the ribs marinate evenly.

Transfer the ribs and all the marinade to the insert of the slow cooker; the marinade will not cover all the ribs. Cover and cook on LOW for 7 to 8 hours. About halfway through the cooking time, carefully reverse the ribs in the insert so that they all cook part of the time in the liquid. The meat is done when it is tender and falling off the bone.

Choucroute Garnie

YIELD: 6 to 8 servings

COOKING TIME: 15 to 20 minutes to cook the meats;
9 to 10 hours for the sauerkraut

16 to 20 assorted sausages of your choice, such as knackwurst, bratwurst, weisswurst, or kielbasa links (see Note)

8 to 10 smoked or fresh pork chops

Vegetable oil, optional

1 recipe Braised Sauerkraut (page 77)

8 to 10 steamed yellow-fleshed potatoes

Assorted mild and spicy mustards

DOES THE AVERAGE FRENCH COOK OWN A SLOW cooker? Not yet, but wait until word gets out that braising the sauerkraut—a time-consuming step for this dish—can be done in the slow cooker with superior texture and as much flavor as the traditional way.

Steam, boil, or grill the sausages, and then cover them and set them aside to keep warm. Sauté the pork chops in hot oil in a large sauté pan until cooked through, or grill them, using the grilling method of your choice.

Mound the hot braised sauerkraut on a large serving platter. Halve the sausages, and then place them on top of the sauerkraut and add the chops and potatoes. Serve hot, accompanied by a variety of mustards.

NOTE: My favorite way to cook the sausages is to place them in a saucepan large enough to hold them comfortably. Add beer to cover. Cover the pan and bring the beer to a low simmer. Cook, covered, until the sausages are cooked through. Cooking time will vary depending on the thickness of the sausage.

Poultry

Chicken Merlot
with Mushrooms

YIELD: 4 to 6 servings

COOKING TIME: 7 to 8 hours on LOW or 3½ to 4 hours on HIGH

SLOW COOKER SIZE: 3½, 4, or 5 quart

2½ to 3 pounds boneless, skinless chicken thighs

12 ounces sliced fresh mushrooms

1 large onion, peeled and chopped

2 garlic cloves, peeled and minced

¾ cup low-sodium chicken broth or Chicken Stock (page 8)

1 (6-ounce) can tomato paste

¼ cup Merlot, or any dry red wine, or additional chicken broth

2 tablespoons quick-cooking tapioca

2 tablespoons chopped fresh basil, or 1½ teaspoons dried basil

2 teaspoons granulated sugar

¼ teaspoon salt

¼ teaspoon freshly ground black pepper

2 cups cooked noodles

2 tablespoons freshly grated Parmesan cheese, preferably Parmigiano-Reggiano

RED WINE AND MUSHROOMS COMPLEMENT THE heartiness of the dark chicken meat. Boneless thighs, available in most supermarkets, make this stew quick to put together.

Rinse the chicken, pat dry, and set aside.

Place the mushrooms, onion, and garlic in the insert of the slow cooker. Place the chicken pieces on top of the vegetables.

Combine the broth, tomato paste, wine, tapioca, dried basil (if using), sugar, salt, and pepper in a medium bowl. Pour the mixture over the chicken and vegetables.

Cover and cook on LOW for 7 to 8 hours or on HIGH for 3½ to 4 hours. If you are using fresh basil, stir it in after the chicken is cooked, shortly before serving. To serve, spoon the chicken, vegetables and sauce over cooked noodles. Sprinkle with Parmesan cheese.

Smoky Stuffed Chicken Breasts

YIELD: 8 servings

COOKING TIME: 6 hours on LOW or 3 to 4 hours on HIGH

SLOW COOKER SIZE: 5$\frac{1}{2}$ to 6 quart

8 large boneless, skinless chicken breast halves

8 slices smoked turkey, cut $\frac{1}{8}$ inch thick

8 ounces smoked Gouda cheese, cut into 8 slices

8 scallions, white part only, cut into 1$\frac{1}{2}$-inch lengths

1 cup low-salt chicken broth or Chicken Stock (page 8)

1 cup canned tomato purée

$\frac{1}{4}$ cup soy sauce

$\frac{1}{3}$ cup packed dark brown sugar

1 to 2 teaspoons finely diced fresh habanero or jalapeño chiles seeded, or dried chiles, reconstituted in hot water, then seeded and diced (see Note)

1 teaspoon smoked paprika (see Note)

$\frac{1}{3}$ cup oil-packed sun-dried tomatoes, drained and diced

Salt and freshly ground black pepper

THINK OF THIS RECIPE WHEN YOU HAVE TO entertain and want to do everything ahead. These freeze beautifully. The subtle smoky flavor is a great match for cornbread and rice with chopped cilantro.

Rinse the chicken breasts and pat dry. Use a sharp knife to lightly score a shallow crosshatch on both sides of each chicken breast half. Lay each breast between two pieces of plastic wrap or waxed paper and use a meat pounder or a heavy saucepan to pound the breasts until they are $\frac{1}{2}$ inch thick. Discard the plastic wrap or waxed paper.

Lay a slice of turkey on each breast half, and then a slice of cheese. Sprinkle some of the scallions over the cheese. Roll each breast into a tight cylinder, tucking the edges in to enclose the filling. Secure the rolls with toothpicks, or wrap each one tightly in cheesecloth. Place the rolls in the insert of the slow cooker in as close to one layer as possible.

Combine the broth, tomato purée, soy sauce, brown sugar, habanero chiles, paprika, and sun-dried tomatoes in a mixing bowl and mix well. Pour this mixture over the chicken. Cover and cook 6 hours on LOW or 3 to 4 hours on HIGH, or until an instant-read thermometer inserted in the center of a breast registers 170°F. Use a slotted spoon to transfer the chicken rolls to a cutting board.

Skim the fat from the cooking liquid, taste, and season with salt and pepper. Remove the toothpicks or cheesecloth from the rolls. Use a sharp knife to slice each roll into 8 pieces, and arrange each sliced breast on a dinner plate so that the slices overlap. Spoon some sauce over and serve.

NOTES: Be sure to wear gloves when you touch hot chiles.

Smoked paprika is made from red peppers that are smoked with oak wood and then ground, giving the product a very distinct, smoky flavor. Look for La Chinata brand, which comes sweet, bittersweet, and hot.

Moroccan Chicken with Prunes and Couscous

YIELD: 4 to 6 servings

COOKING TIME: 4 to 5 hours on LOW

SLOW COOKER SIZE: 4 quart

FOR THE CHICKEN

2½ to 3 pounds chicken parts, skinned

1 tablespoon vegetable oil

1 cup (7 ounces) pitted prunes

2 large onions, peeled and sliced

2 teaspoons whole cumin seeds

1½ cups low-sodium chicken broth or Chicken Stock (page 8)

2 tablespoons minced garlic

2 tablespoons peeled and minced fresh ginger

1 teaspoon ground turmeric

1 teaspoon ground cinnamon

¾ teaspoon salt

¼ teaspoon freshly ground black pepper

FOR THE COUSCOUS AND GARNISH

1½ cups (10 ounces) uncooked couscous

ANOTHER WINNER ON EMMY'S HIT PARADE. THE flavors meld together to create a succulent, sweet-and-savory dish with tremendous flavor. This is a terrific party dish—everyone loves it!

Rinse the chicken pieces well and pat dry. Brown them in the oil in a large skillet over medium-high heat for about 2 minutes per side; you may have to brown the chicken in two batches. Transfer to the insert of the slow cooker, and tuck the prunes among the chicken pieces. Add the onions and cumin seeds to the skillet and cook, stirring, over medium-high heat for about 5 minutes, until the onions are soft and the seeds are fragrant. Pour in the broth and add the garlic, ginger, turmeric, cinnamon, salt, and pepper. Bring the mixture to a boil, stir well, and pour it over the chicken and prunes. Cover and cook on LOW for 4½ hours, or until the chicken is very tender. Use a slotted spoon to transfer the chicken pieces, prunes, and onions to a serving platter; mound them in the center of the platter and keep warm by loosely covering the dish with aluminum foil.

Measure 2 cups of the cooking liquid into a medium saucepan and bring to a boil. Add the couscous, stir, cover, and remove the saucepan from the heat. Let stand for 5 minutes, and then fluff the couscous with a fork. Arrange it around the chicken on the platter,

1 teaspoon peeled and minced fresh ginger

¼ cup chopped fresh cilantro

⅓ cup chopped toasted slivered almonds, chopped (see Note)

and sprinkle the chicken with the ginger, cilantro, and almonds. Pour over any leftover cooking juices.

NOTE: To toast almonds, place them on a rimmed baking sheet and toast them in a preheated 350°F oven for 8 to 10 minutes, until they are light golden brown and fragrant.

Braised Pheasant

YIELD: 4 servings

COOKING TIME: 3 to 5 hours on HIGH

SLOW COOKER SIZE: 5½-quart oval

1 medium onion, peeled and sliced

½ cup all-purpose flour

1 teaspoon salt

1 teaspoon freshly ground black pepper

1 (3½- to 4-pound) pheasant, cut into 4 pieces, rinsed, and patted dry

2 to 3 tablespoons olive oil

1½ cups dry red wine, or more if needed

1 cup low-sodium chicken broth or Chicken Stock (page 8)

2 teaspoons fresh thyme leaves

2 bay leaves

WHEN MY FRIEND ROSE MARY SCHAEFER WENT to Paris to study cooking, I asked her to look for recipes that could be adapted to the slow cooker. She introduced me to this deep, rich pheasant ragoût that will make you believe you stepped into a Parisian bistro. Serve with roasted potatoes.

Strew the onion in the bottom of the insert of the slow cooker. On a plate, mix the flour with ½ teaspoon of the salt and ½ teaspoon of the pepper. Dredge the pheasant pieces In the seasoned flour. Heat 2 tablespoons of olive oil in a large sauté pan over medium-high heat, and brown the pheasant pieces in the hot oil. Place them in the insert. You may have to brown them in batches, and you may need to add more oil as you work.

Pour 1½ cups of wine and the broth into the sauté pan and bring to a boil over high heat, scraping up the browned bits of meat clinging to the pan with a wooden spoon. Pour the mixture over the pheasant, and add enough more wine to come two thirds of the way up the meat. Add the thyme leaves, bay leaves, the remaining ½ teaspoon salt, and the remaining ½ teaspoon pepper.

Cover and cook on HIGH for 3 hours, until the thigh juices run clear when pierced with the tip of a small knife, the meat starts to fall off the bones, and an instant-read thermometer inserted in the thigh registers 180°F. Drain the cooking liquid into a small saucepan, remove the bay leaves, skim off any fat, and add additional salt and pepper to taste, if desired. Bring the liquid to a low simmer while you remove the skin from the pheasant. Place the meat on a serving platter or divide it among four dinner plates. Spoon the hot cooking liquid over and serve.

Braised Duck

YIELD: about 4 cups of duck meat

COOKING TIME: 6 to 8 hours on HIGH

SLOW COOKER SIZE: 4 quart

1 (4-pound) duck

6 unpeeled garlic cloves

10 sprigs fresh rosemary

10 sprigs fresh thyme

2 large carrots, peeled and cut in 4 pieces

1 cup low-sodium chicken broth or Chicken Stock (page 8)

Coarse salt

Freshly ground black pepper

B RAISING DUCK IN THE SLOW COOKER IS A GREAT way to have tender, succulent meat for salad or an elegant pasta sauce. The addition of garlic, thyme, and rosemary perfume the air with the aromas of Provence.

Remove the giblets from the duck cavity and reserve them for another use, if desired. Rinse the duck inside and out with cool water, and pat dry. Place the garlic, rosemary, and thyme inside the duck cavity and place the duck, breast side down, in the insert of the slow cooker. Strew the carrots around the duck, pour in the broth, and sprinkle the duck with salt and pepper. Cover and cook on HIGH for 6 to 8 hours, turning the duck breast side up halfway through the cooking time. When the meat is very tender, turn off the slow cooker and allow the duck to cool, covered, for 15 minutes.

Use two large slotted spoons to transfer the duck to a shallow bowl. When the duck is cool enough to handle, remove the meat from the bones. Strain the stock into a bowl and discard the carrots and herbs. Reserve the cooked garlic to make the salad dressing on page 138. Place the bowl of stock in the refrigerator until it has cooled and the fat has congealed. Skim off the fat and reserve it, if desired, for other uses, such as sautéing potatoes and for

Duck Confit (page 138). Place the stock in plastic containers, cover, and refrigerate for 3 days or freeze for up to 3 months. The stock can be used for Civet de Canard (page 135) or Cassoulet (page 137), or as the base for any soup with duck meat. Use the duck meat in Duck and Red Potato Salad (page 134), Braised Duck with Bow Tie Pasta (page 131), or Duck Pâté (page 39).

Braised Duck with Bow Tie Pasta

YIELD: 6 to 8 servings

COOKING TIME: 20 minutes for the pasta; 6 to 8 hours for the duck

1 pound dried bow tie pasta

1½ tablespoons olive oil

2 shallots, peeled and minced

½ cup full-bodied dry red wine, such as Merlot

½ cup canned chicken broth, braising liquid from Braised Duck (page 129), or Chicken Stock (page 8)

3 to 4 garlic cloves from Braised Duck, squeezed to release the pulp

2 cups duck meat from Braised Duck

1 cup fresh corn kernels or frozen corn, defrosted slightly

Salt and freshly ground black pepper

I LIKE TO KEEP SOME BRAISED DUCK MEAT (PAGE 129) in the freezer so I can whip it out and make this hearty cold-weather pasta dish when the first snow hits New England. I like to think it helps me shovel the driveway faster so I can get those cross-country skis on and start having some fun.

Bring a large pot of salted water to a rapid boil and cook the pasta according to the package directions.

Meanwhile, heat the oil in a large sauté pan over medium-high heat. Sauté the shallots until soft. Whisk in the wine, broth, and garlic pulp, using the whisk to mash the garlic. Increase the heat and bring the mixture to a rapid boil, stirring constantly, until it is reduced by one third. Add the duck meat and corn, lower the heat, and cook just until the corn is hot. Add salt and pepper to taste.

Drain the pasta, reserving about ½ cup of the cooking water. Use the water to thin the duck sauce, if necessary. Divide the pasta among 6 or 8 bowls, and then spoon on the sauce.

Duck Breast with Preserved Quince

YIELD: 2 servings

COOKING TIME: 15 minutes; 8 to 12 hours for the preserved quince

2 boneless duck breast halves

Salt and freshly ground black pepper

2 to 3 cups mesclun salad greens, washed and patted dry

Vinaigrette dressing of your choice

3 to 4 tablespoons Preserved Quince in Cinnamon Syrup (recipe follows)

THIS IS AN ELEGANT COLD STARTER OR LIGHT main course. The contrast of the savory duck breast and sweet quince is unusual but surprisingly good.

Use a sharp knife to score a crosshatch through the skin and fat layer of each duck breast half, and then season with salt and pepper. Heat a medium sauté pan over medium-high heat. When it is very hot, place the breast halves skin side down in the pan and cook for about 4 minutes. Remove the breasts from the pan, discard the accumulated fat, and then place the breasts back in the pan, skin side up. Cook for 4 to 6 minutes more, until the meat is cooked but still slightly rosy inside, or to desired doneness. Transfer the meat to a plate and set aside.

Divide the greens between 2 plates and drizzle with some of the vinaigrette. Place a breast half on each serving of greens, and spoon some of the preserved quince on the duck. Drizzle each serving with a little more vinaigrette.

Preserved Quince in Cinnamon Syrup

Yield: about 10 cups of fruit and syrup

Cooking time: 8 to 12 hours on HIGH

Slow cooker size: 4 quart

3 pounds fresh quinces
(about 3 large quinces)

6 cups granulated sugar

1 cup orange juice or water

1 cinnamon stick, 3 inches long

1 lemon, well scrubbed, halved, seeded, and thinly sliced

A GOLDEN QUINCE LOOKS LIKE A CROSS BETWEEN a fat-bottomed pear and a Golden Delicious apple. Available fresh in the fall months, quinces are rock hard and are rarely eaten raw. High in natural fruit jelly, or pectin, they are the perfect thing for preserves. While the flesh is rather pale and anemic, it turns a gorgeous ruby red color during the cooking process. Spoon it over ice cream or pound cake, or eat it as is.

The combination of the sweet quince and savory duck breast is sublime.

Do not peel the quinces. Use a heavy chef's knife to cut each in half. Use a teaspoon to scoop and scrape out the seeds. Cut the fruit into 1-inch slices, and then into 1-inch cubes. Place the quinces, sugar, orange juice or water, cinnamon stick, and lemon in the insert of the slow cooker. Cover and cook on HIGH for 8 to 12 hours, or until the fruit is very soft. Spoon the fruit into sterilized jars, cover with syrup, and refrigerate. Serve over ice cream, pound cake, pancakes, waffles, or French toast.

Store the quince and syrup in tightly sealed jars in the refrigerator where it will keep for 3 to 4 months.

Duck and Red Potato Salad

YIELD: 8 servings

COOKING TIME: 20 minutes for the beans and potatoes; 6 to 8 hours for the duck

FOR THE DRESSING

4 garlic cloves reserved from Braised Duck, cold or reheated gently in a saucepan or in a microwave oven

1/3 cup red wine vinegar

1 tablespoon packed dark brown sugar

1 tablespoon Dijon mustard

1 tablespoon soy sauce

3/4 cup olive oil

Salt

FOR THE SALAD

8 cups mesclun salad greens, washed and dried

1 pound thin French green beans (*haricots verts*), trimmed, blanched in boiling water until cooked but still crunchy, and then drained and patted dry

16 medium Red Bliss potatoes, steamed until tender, cooled, and quartered

1 recipe Braised Duck (page 129)

1 medium red onion, peeled and very thinly sliced

THIS IS THE ULTIMATE POTATO SALAD. SERVE IT cold or reheat the duck before adding it to the greens. I like to heat the duck quickly in a sauté pan before I add it to the top of the greens in this salad.

To make the dressing, place the garlic pulp in a mixing bowl and mash it with a wire whisk. Whisk in the vinegar, brown sugar, mustard, and soy sauce. Add the olive oil slowly and whisk until it emulsifies. Add salt or additional soy sauce to taste. Set aside.

To assemble individual salads, place about 1 cup of greens on each of 8 salad plates. Place some green beans and potatoes on the greens, and then place some duck meat in a small pile on top. Scatter the onion rounds over all. Whisk the dressing to blend, and drizzle over the salads just before serving.

Civet de Canard

YIELD: 4 servings

COOKING TIME: 6 to 8 hours on LOW

SLOW COOKER SIZE: 5½ or 6 quart

2 whole duck breasts, split (about 5 pounds total)

12 ounces thickly cut bacon, preferably smoked, each slice cut into ½-inch squares

3 shallots, peeled and finely chopped

5 garlic cloves, peeled and minced

¼ cup all-purpose flour

1 cup duck stock from Braised Duck (page 129), or low-sodium beef broth

2 cups dry red wine

2 large carrots, peeled and finely chopped

2 bay leaves

1 heaping tablespoon chopped fresh rosemary leaves

1 heaping tablespoon fresh thyme leaves

1 tablespoon fresh marjoram leaves

1 teaspoon salt

1 teaspoon freshly ground black pepper

IN PARIS, TUCKED AWAY BEHIND NOTRE DAME, IS a restaurant called *Le Vieux Bistro* ("The Old Bistro"). Its signature dish is duck stewed in red wine with garlic and a mix of herbs from the French countryside. Accompany this dish with a loaf of crusty French bread, and wash it down with a great Burgundy, and you can experience a sensory trip to France without leaving your house. A 5½- or 6-quart oval slow cooker is ideal for this.

Rinse the duck breasts under cool running water and pat dry. Use a small, sharp knife to score the duck skin at 1-inch intervals. In a large sauté pan set over high heat, sauté the duck breasts until browned on all sides, and then place them in the insert of the slow cooker.

Discard the fat in the sauté pan and cook the bacon over medium heat until crisp. Use a slotted spoon to transfer the bacon to the slow cooker insert. Discard all but a few tablespoons of the bacon fat, and sauté the shallots and garlic over low heat until softened. Sprinkle with the flour and cook, stirring, over medium heat, for 1 minute. Pour in the stock or broth and wine and bring to a boil, scraping up the browned bits of meat clinging to the pan with a wooden spoon. Pour into the slow cooker insert. Add the carrots, bay leaves, rosemary, thyme, marjoram, salt, and pepper.

Cover and cook on LOW for 6 hours, or until the meat is tender when pierced with a sharp knife. Use a slotted spoon to remove the duck to a serving platter. Remove and discard the skin. Keep the meat warm by covering the platter loosely with a large sheet of aluminum foil.

Strain the cooking liquid into a large saucepan and skim off the fat. Bring the liquid to a boil over high heat and reduce to about 2 cups. Season with salt and pepper and spoon over the duck. Serve with polenta or Garlic Smashed Potatoes (page 72).

Cassoulet

YIELD: 8 servings

COOKING TIME: 6 hours on LOW or 3 hours on HIGH for the cassoulet;
5 to 9 hours for the confit

SLOW COOKER SIZE: 5½ to 6 quart

1 pound dried flageolets or lima beans, rinsed, drained, and picked over to remove dirt or debris

3 celery stalks, cut into 2-inch lengths

3 large carrots, peeled and cut into 1-inch lengths

4 garlic cloves, crushed and peeled

3 cups Caramelized Onions (page 10) and 1 cup of their cooking liquid, or 2 large Spanish onions, peeled and cut into thick slices

1 bay leaf

4 to 5 cups chicken broth, beef broth, Chicken Stock (page 8), or stock from Braised Duck (page 129) plus broth or other stock

1 tablespoon dried *herbes de Provence* (see Note)

Salt and black pepper

1 recipe Duck Confit (recipe follows), skin, bones, and cooking fat removed, meat shredded

THIS TRADITIONAL HEARTY FRENCH CLASSIC might be thought of as baked beans, French style. While they make it with goose confit (preserved goose) in France, this version from Lora Brody's *Plugged In* is made with duck confit. The confit must be made a day ahead.

Place the beans, celery, carrots, garlic, onions, bay leaf, broth, *herbes de Provence*, and salt and pepper to taste in the insert of the slow cooker. Cover and cook on LOW for 6 hours or on HIGH for 3 hours, until the beans are very soft but not falling apart. Add the shredded duck meat and cook long enough to heat it through. Discard the bay leaf before serving.

NOTE: If you cannot find *herbes de Provence*, you can make your own by combining equal amounts of dried tarragon, rosemary, chervil, basil, and thyme leaves.

Duck Confit

Yield: 1½ pounds (about 3 cups) duck meat

Cooking time: 1 hour on HIGH, then 4 to 8 hours on LOW, for a total of 5 to 9 hours

Slow cooker size: 5½ to 6 quart

2 whole duck breasts, split

1½ pounds rendered duck, goose, or chicken fat (see Note)

6 garlic cloves, peeled

1 large shallot, peeled and coarsely chopped

1 tablespoon kosher salt

2 teaspoons freshly ground black pepper

1 tablespoon dried *herbes de Provence* (see Note)

CONFIT IS AN AGE-OLD METHOD OF PRESERVING duck, goose, or other meats for winter consumption. The meat is salted and slowly simmered in its own fat. Most of the heavy fat is absorbed by the meat, leaving the meat unbelievably tender. When the confit is done, the meat is put in crocks and sealed with fat for storage.

Modern refrigeration and freezers have eliminated the need for confit as a preservation method. The taste and the unique tenderness that result from this cooking technique are what we're after here, and the slow cooker is the perfect vehicle for delivering it. Duck lends itself readily to this recipe, as does the traditional goose.

Place the duck breasts in the insert of the slow cooker and add the fat, garlic, shallot, salt, pepper, and *herbes de Provence*. Cover, set the slow cooker on HIGH, and cook for 1 hour. Reduce the heat to LOW and cook until the duck is very, very tender—at least 4 and up to 8 hours. Use a slotted spoon to remove the duck from the fat, which can be strained, frozen, and reused. Serve the duck hot or at room temperature, or use it to make cassoulet.

NOTES: You can buy canned goose fat in gourmet food stores. If you have not accumulated your own duck or goose fat, chicken fat is perfectly acceptable.

There are three ways to get chicken fat for this recipe: You can skim congealed fat off the top of chicken soup or stock, buy it in a plastic tub from a kosher butcher, or make it yourself. To make your own, place raw chicken fat in a heavy saucepan and cook very slowly over medium-low heat until the fat has melted, the connective tissue has darkened and crisped, and any water has evaporated. Strain the rendered fat into a bowl. Rendered chicken fat can be kept in a sealed container in the freezer for up to 6 months.

If you cannot find *herbes de Provence*, you can make your own by combining equal amounts of dried tarragon, rosemary, chervil, basil, and thyme leaves.

Fish

Slow Cooked Salmon

YIELD: 4 servings

COOKING TIME: 1½ hours on HIGH

SLOW COOKER SIZE: 5½- to 6-quart oval

4 salmon steaks (about 6 ounces each)

½ cup strained fresh lime juice

3 tablespoons cognac

2 tablespoons granulated sugar

1 tablespoon kosher salt

1 teaspoon finely ground white pepper

1 large bunch fresh dill, rinsed and dried

2 tablespoons olive oil

Mustard Dill Sauce, optional (recipe follows)

WHEN I READ THAT SOME RED-HOT CHEF IN New York was roasting salmon in a 200°F oven for 6 hours and charging thirty dollars for it, I knew I could produce the same results in my slow cooker. The salmon must be marinated for 24 to 48 hours before it is ready to cook.

To marinate the salmon, lay a generous length of heavy-duty aluminum foil on a work surface. In a small bowl whisk together the lime juice and cognac. Rub both sides of each steak with the mixture. In another small bowl or ramekin, combine the sugar, salt, and pepper. Rub both sides of each steak with about 2 teaspoons of this mixture. Lay half the fresh dill in the center of the foil and place the steaks side by side on top of the dill. Lay the remaining dill on top of the steaks. Pull the foil over the salmon and seal it to form a tight package. Place the package on a rimmed baking sheet or in a shallow roasting pan. Cover the foil package with a plate or lid and put a weight on top, such as an unopened half-gallon carton of milk. Refrigerate for at least 24 and up to 48 hours.

Thirty minutes before you plan to cook the salmon, pour the oil into the insert of the slow cooker and preheat it on HIGH with the cover on. Remove the salmon from the foil and discard the dill. Use a damp paper towel to gently wipe the seasonings off the fish.

Place the steaks in one layer in the slow cooker. Cook on HIGH for 90 minutes, and then check the temperature of one steak with an instant-read thermometer. It should register 140°F when inserted in the center. (Be sure to wait 90 minutes to do this; lifting the lid allows the heat to escape, which slows the cooking process.) Serve the salmon hot with Mustard Dill Sauce or cold with an herbed mayonnaise.

Mustard Dill Sauce

½ cup Dijon mustard

2 tablespoons soy sauce

⅓ cup packed dark brown sugar

3 tablespoons olive oil

⅓ cup chopped fresh dill

Whisk together all the ingredients in a small bowl. Spoon the sauce over the fish just before serving.

Fish Roulades with Tomatillo Salsa

Yield: 6 servings

Cooking time: 30 minutes for the fish; 1½ to 2 hours for the salsa

2 tablespoons mild olive oil or vegetable oil

12 small skinless fillets of sole (about 2¼ pounds total)

12 large sea scallops, rinsed and patted dry, tough connective tissue removed

½ cup dry white wine

4 cups Tomatillo Salsa with Peppers (page 24)

USE SMALL FILLETS OF SOLE, COD, OR HADDOCK to make this beautifully colored and wonderful-tasting dish. I like to serve it with Garlic Smashed Potatoes (page 72). This can also be served as a cold appetizer or entrée.

Preheat the oven to 375°F with a rack in the upper third, but not in the highest position. Lightly coat a shallow ovenproof 9-inch by 13-inch baking dish with olive oil. Lay one fish fillet on a work surface. Place a scallop at one end of the fillet, and roll the fillet around the scallop to enclose it. Repeat with the remaining fillets and scallops, and then place the rolls close together, on their sides, in the baking dish.

Pour the wine into the baking dish, and then spoon the salsa over the fish roulades. Bake in the upper third of the oven for 30 minutes, or until the sauce bubbles and the fish flakes easily with a fork. Serve hot with the Garlic Smashed Potatoes (page 76) or cold with a rice salad.

Sole with Pine Nuts

YIELD: 4 servings

COOKING TIME: 2 hours on HIGH

SLOW COOKER SIZE: 4½-quart oval

4 tablespoons butter

2 shallots, peeled and minced

4 tablespoons pine nuts

1¼ cups fresh bread crumbs made from firm-textured French or Italian bread

1 tablespoon Dijon mustard

1 tablespoon soy sauce

¼ cup minced fresh flat-leaf parsley, plus about ¼ cup chopped parsley for garnish

2 tablespoons strained fresh lemon juice

8 fillets of sole (1¾ to 2 pounds total)

ENCLOSED, MOIST HEAT GIVES A FLAKY TENDERness to fish dishes, while retaining their flavor. You can use any white, delicately flavored fish fillet, but I like the texture of sole the best.

Set the slow cooker on HIGH. Place 2 tablespoons of the butter in the insert and heat, covered, for 30 minutes. (This step is to heat up the insert so the fish cooks more efficiently.) Melt the remaining 2 tablespoons butter in a small sauté pan set over moderate heat. Cook the shallots, stirring frequently, until they are soft. Add the pine nuts and continue cooking, stirring frequently, until they are golden. Remove to a small mixing bowl. Add the bread crumbs, mustard, soy sauce, minced parsley, and lemon juice. Mix thoroughly.

Place 2 tablespoons of the stuffing on the narrow end of each sole fillet. Roll each fillet like a jelly roll, and place, seam side down, in the warm, buttered insert. Cover and cook on HIGH for 2 hours, or until fish flakes when pierced with a fork. Use a slotted spoon to transfer the fish to dinner plates. Garnish with the chopped parsley, and serve with rice or boiled potatoes.

Slow Cooker Scallops

Yield: 2 servings

Cooking time: 30 to 40 minutes on HIGH

Slow cooker size: 3½ quart

1 tablespoon butter

4 thin slices lemon

1 large garlic clove, peeled and halved lengthwise

8 to 10 ounces bay scallops or sea scallops (half or quarter sea scallops), rinsed and patted dry, tough connective tissue removed

⅛ teaspoon kosher salt

Freshly ground black pepper

¼ cup chopped fresh flat-leaf parsley

2 lemon wedges

THANKS TO MY WEB SITE (WWW.LORABRODY. com) I get to "talk" to hundreds of home cooks. When word got out that I was writing a slow cooker book, Char Roberts generously offered to try her hand at scallops. The results were amazing! Tender, succulent, and flavorful, these scallops are among the best I've ever tasted. I'm sure all my readers will join me in thanking Char for discovering yet another unique use for the slow cooker.

Place the butter, lemon slices, and garlic in the insert of the slow cooker. Set on HIGH, cover, and heat until the butter is hot, about 30 minutes. Add the scallops and sprinkle with the salt. Stir to coat them with the butter and seasonings, cover, and cook on HIGH for 30 to 40 minutes, or until the scallops are thoroughly hot and opaque in the center.

To serve, press the lemon slices with the back of a spoon to release their juices, and then discard them. Sprinkle the scallops and their cooking liquid with freshly ground black pepper to taste. Use a slotted spoon to transfer the scallops to 2 serving plates. Drizzle each serving with some of the cooking liquid, sprinkle with chopped parsley, and serve with fresh lemon wedges.

Pasta, Breads, and Grains

Pasta Fazool

YIELD: 6 servings

COOKING TIME: 4½ hours on HIGH

SLOW COOKER SIZE: 4 quart

FOR THE BEANS AND PASTA

1 pound dried cannellini beans, rinsed, drained, and picked over to remove any bits of dirt and debris

1 (28-ounce) can whole peeled tomatoes and juice, roughly chopped

3½ cups low-sodium beef broth

1 medium onion, peeled and chopped

1 medium carrot, peeled and cut into ¼-inch dice

2 garlic cloves, peeled and chopped

2 sprigs fresh rosemary

6 sprigs fresh flat-leaf parsley

½ teaspoon fennel seeds, crushed (see Note)

1 teaspoon dried thyme

¼ teaspoon freshly ground black pepper

1 teaspoon salt

BEANS AND PASTA MAKE A WINNING COMBINA-tion. The meaty cannellini beans are perfect for this dish, and the small pasta shells trap the cooking juices so well. A hit of fresh rosemary sprinkled on at the end is tasty, or, even better, try a swirl of Rosemary-Infused Oil (page 16), garlic-flavored oil from Caramelized Garlic (page 40), or extra-virgin olive oil.

Place the beans in the insert of the slow cooker. Pour the toma-toes over them, and add the broth, onion, carrot, garlic, rosemary and parsley sprigs, fennel seeds, thyme, pepper, and salt. Stir well, and then cover and cook on HIGH for 4½ hours, or until the beans are cooked but not mushy. Taste, and add more salt and pepper, if needed. Turn off the slow cooker and stir in the spinach leaves. Cover and let the mixture sit while you cook the pasta.

Cook the pasta in a large pot of boiling water. Drain well and return the pasta to the pot. Pour in the beans and sauce and stir well. Ladle out portions into large, shallow bowls, and garnish as desired.

10 ounces baby spinach leaves, well rinsed and patted dry

1 pound small pasta, such as tiny shells (less than ½-inch long)

OPTIONAL GARNISHES (USE SOME OR ALL)

2 tablespoons chopped fresh flat-leaf parsley

1 tablespoon minced fresh rosemary

2 slices bacon, cooked and crumbled

Freshly grated Parmesan cheese, preferably Parmigiano-Reggiano

About 3 tablespoons Rosemary-Infused Oil (page 16), oil from Caramelized Garlic (page 40), or extra-virgin olive oil

NOTE: Crush fennel seeds with a mortar and pestle, or place them in a small resealable plastic bag and crush them with a rolling pin or meat pounder.

Pasta with Caramelized Garlic and Fresh Parsley

YIELD: 6 servings

COOKING TIME: 5 to 15 minutes for the pasta; 5 to 8 hours for the caramelized garlic

1½ pounds pasta of your choice, fresh or dried

5 to 6 cloves Caramelized Garlic (page 40)

⅓ cup garlic oil from Caramelized Garlic

1 cup chopped fresh flat-leaf parsley

Salt and freshly ground black pepper to taste

Freshly grated Parmesan cheese, preferably Parmigiano-Reggiano

WITH SOME CARAMELIZED GARLIC ON HAND, this hearty pasta dish is a snap to make.

Cook the pasta in rapidly boiling salted water until al dente. Drain, reserving ½ cup of the cooking water. Place the pasta in a warmed bowl. Squeeze the pulp out of the garlic cloves into the pasta, and add the garlic oil, parsley, salt, and pepper. Toss, add some of the reserved cooking water, if necessary, and serve. Pass the cheese separately.

Penne with Spicy Onion Sauce

YIELD: 6 servings

COOKING TIME: 9 to 10 hours on LOW

SLOW COOKER SIZE: 4 quart

¼ cup vegetable oil

3 garlic cloves, peeled and minced

3 pounds Spanish onions, peeled and thinly sliced (about 12 cups)

2 large leeks, white parts only, halved lengthwise, rinsed well, and thinly sliced into semicircles

2 to 4 bottled hot cherry peppers, stemmed, seeded, and finely chopped

2 to 4 tablespoons pickling liquid from bottle of cherry peppers

1 pound dried penne pasta

3 to 4 links sweet Italian sausage, cooked and cut into ¼-inch-thick slices, optional

Salt and freshly ground black pepper to taste

½ cup chopped fresh flat-leaf parsley

About ½ cup freshly grated Parmesan cheese, preferably Parmigiano-Reggiano

THIS SPICY PASTA DISH PROMISES TO HEAT UP the coldest winter day. The red cherry peppers add a nice muted color to the sauce, even after a long simmer in the slow cooker. Both the peppers and their pickling liquid are very hot, so taste them carefully before starting to cook. The optional sausage rounds out this dish to make it a complete meal.

Heat the oil in a small sauté pan over medium heat and sauté the garlic until softened. Scrape it into the insert of the slow cooker. (If your microwave oven is large enough to hold the slow cooker insert, place the oil and garlic in the insert of the slow cooker, cover with the inverted lid or a flat plate, place the insert in the microwave, and cook on HIGH for 4 to 5 minutes, or until the garlic has softened.)

Place the onions, leeks, cherry peppers, and the pickling liquid in the insert of the slow cooker. Use two forks to toss the ingredients together, and then cover and cook on LOW for 9 to 10 hours, until the onions are deep golden brown and tender. They will cook down considerably.

When ready to serve, cook the pasta in a large pot of boiling water according to package directions. Drain well and reserve about ½ cup of the cooking water. Return the drained pasta to the pot and stir in the onion and pepper sauce and the optional cooked sausage. If the dish seems dry, add some of the pasta water. Toss well and season with salt and pepper to taste. (Remember that adding cheese will add salt.) Serve in shallow bowls, and sprinkle each serving with some parsley and cheese.

Black Bean Bread

YIELD: 1 large loaf

COOKING TIME: 35 to 40 minutes for the bread;
12 to 18 hours for the frijoles negros

FOR PREPARING THE DOUGH

1 tablespoon active dry yeast,
(not rapid rise)

½ cup yellow cornmeal

3 tablespoons Lora Brody's
Dough Relaxer™, optional

2 cups all-purpose flour

1 cup whole wheat flour

1 tablespoon Lora Brody's Bread
Dough Enhancer™, optional

1½ teaspoons salt

2 teaspoons chili powder

1 cup Frijoles Negros (page 14)

¼ cup vegetable oil

1 extra-large egg

1 tablespoon honey

⅔ cup water, plus additional
water if necessary to make a
smooth soft ball of dough after
the first five minutes of kneading

WHEN YOU COMBINE LEGUMES AND GRAINS, the result is a perfect protein; this fragrant loaf is good for you and has the added benefit of being wonderfully tasty. The Bread Dough Relaxer™ gives a softer crumb and crust, plus a calcium boost. The Bread Dough Enhancer™ helps this rather dense loaf rise higher and increases its shelf life as well. It is available by mail order from the King Arthur Flour Baker's Catalogue (800-827-6836; www.kingarthurflour.com) and from my Web site (www.lorabrody.com). This dough can also be used for the Tomatillo Salsa Pizza on page 157.

Place all of the ingredients for the dough in a mixing bowl, in the work bowl of a heavy-duty electric mixer fitted with a dough hook, in a bread machine programmed for DOUGH, or in the work bowl of a food processor fitted with the plastic blade. Knead by hand or with the mixer for 7 to 9 minutes; knead in the bread machine until the control panel indicates the end of the dough cycle; or process in the food processor for two 2-minute periods with a 2-minute rest in between. You may need to add extra water after 5 minutes of kneading. Whichever method you use, work the dough until a soft, smooth discrete ball forms.

Allow the dough to rise until doubled in bulk. If kneaded by hand, place the dough in a clean bowl; for the other methods, leave the dough in the mixer bowl, food processor bowl, or bread machine.

FOR BAKING THE BREAD

2 tablespoons yellow cornmeal

1 extra-large egg white

2 tablespoons water

Pinch of salt

When it has doubled, punch it down and place it on a lightly floured work surface to rest for 5 minutes.

To prepare the dough for baking, cover a heavy-duty baking sheet with foil or parchment paper and sprinkle it with the 2 tablespoons of cornmeal. Form the dough into a low dome about 9 inches in diameter and 3 inches high in the center. Mix together the egg white, water, and salt in a small bowl. Brush the dough with the egg wash and allow to rise on the baking sheet, uncovered, until doubled in bulk.

Preheat the oven to 375°F with a rack in the center position. Bake the loaf on this rack for 35 to 40 minutes, or until an instant-read thermometer inserted in the center registers 200°F. Cool completely before slicing.

Slow Cooker
Sticky Bun Bread

YIELD: 1 large loaf

COOKING TIME: 45 minutes

SLOW COOKER SIZE: 3 to 4 quart

FOR THE DOUGH

1 tablespoon active dry yeast (not rapid rise)

3 tablespoons granulated sugar

1½ teaspoons salt

3 tablespoons Lora Brody's Bread Dough Relaxer™, optional

⅓ cup vegetable oil

⅔ cup water, plus extra to make a smooth, soft ball during the first 5 minutes of kneading

3 cups all-purpose flour, plus extra as needed

2 tablespoons unsalted butter, softened

FOR THE FILLING

3 tablespoons unsalted butter, softened

1½ cups raisins

1 cup toasted pecans or walnuts, chopped

I HAD A HUNCH THAT YOU COULD USE THE SLOW cooker as a dough proofer—a place to let bread dough rise—and it's true. The slow cooker is perfect because it's a warm, enclosed environment. The fact is, you can even place the insert in the oven and bake the bread in it. Of course, you do end up with a loaf of round bread, but in the case of these delicious sticky buns, the shape is perfect.

To make the dough, place the yeast, sugar, salt, optional dough relaxer, oil, ⅔ cup water, and 3 cups flour in a large mixing bowl. Stir the ingredients together with a wooden spoon, and then turn the dough out onto a lightly floured work surface. Knead the dough gently, adding additional water or flour to form a soft, supple ball of dough.

Use the butter to generously coat the inside of the slow cooker insert. Cover the insert and turn the slow cooker on HIGH for 5 minutes, or just until the insert feels warm to the touch, and then turn it off. Place the dough in the insert and cover. Allow it to rise until doubled in bulk.

While the dough is rising, toss the filling ingredients together with a fork in a medium mixing bowl. Set aside.

When the dough has doubled in bulk, transfer it to a lightly floured work surface. Cover the empty slow cooker and heat on HIGH for 5 minutes to rewarm the insert, and then turn it off. There

⅔ cup packed dark brown sugar

1 tablespoon ground cinnamon

FOR THE TOPPING

1 cup confectioners' sugar

2 tablespoons unsalted butter, softened

3 to 4 tablespoons hot water

1 tablespoon pure vanilla extract

should still be a coating of butter on the sides of the insert. If not, coat it with more butter.

Use a rolling pin to roll the dough into a rectangle about 24 inches long and 8 inches wide. Scatter the filling mixture over the surface. Start with a long edge and roll the dough, jelly-roll style, to form a 24-inch-long roll. Try not to stretch the dough as you roll. Curl the roll into a tight spiral and place it in the warmed slow cooker insert. Cover the slow cooker and allow the dough to rise until almost doubled in bulk.

Preheat the oven to 350°F with a rack in the lower third, but not lowest position. (To accommodate the insert, you may have to remove the other shelves.) Place the insert, uncovered, in the oven and bake for 40 to 45 minutes, until the crust is well browned and an instant-read thermometer inserted in the center of the rolls registers 200°F.

While the loaf is baking, make the topping. Put the confectioners' sugar, butter, 3 tablespoons of water, and vanilla extract in a small bowl and stir with a fork until smooth. Add just enough water, if necessary, so that the topping flows slowly off the fork.

When the loaf is done, remove the insert from the oven and immediately invert the contents onto a wire rack. Immediately invert the loaf again onto a serving plate and spoon the topping over it. Cut the loaf into wedges and serve warm or at room temperature.

Tomatillo Salsa Pizza

YIELD: 8 servings

COOKING TIME: about 30 minutes for the pizza; 1½ to 2 hours for the salsa

1 package pizza dough, white bread dough, or 1 recipe dough for Black Bean Bread (page 153)

8 ounces whipped cream cheese, at room temperature

2 to 3 cups Tomatillo Salsa with Peppers (page 24)

2 cups shredded Cheddar or Monterey Jack cheese

I MAKE A VARIATION OF THIS FOR SUPER BOWL every year. No matter how exciting the game, this pizza is always appreciated; and, judging by how quickly the slices go, it is definitely a crowd pleaser. You can use store-bought pizza dough, white bread dough, or the dough recipe for Black Bean Bread (page 153).

Roll the dough out to fit an 11- by 17-inch heavy-duty rimmed baking sheet or a round deep-dish pizza pan about 14 inches in diameter. Place the dough in the pan, cover with plastic wrap or a clean kitchen towel, and allow to rise in a warm place until puffy and nearly double in bulk.

Preheat the oven to 425°F with a rack at the center position. Drop the cream cheese by teaspoonfuls evenly over the surface of the dough, and then gently spread it with a rubber spatula, trying not to deflate the dough too much. It isn't necessary to be too neat or to cover the dough completely—the cheese will melt and spread as the pizza bakes. Spoon the salsa on top, and then sprinkle with shredded cheese.

Bake for 15 minutes at 425°F, and then reduce the oven temperature to 375°F and bake until the top is bubbling and the dough is no longer raw in the center. (Check by using a small sharp knife to cut into the center.) Serve hot, warm, or at room temperature, with plenty of cold beer.

Chestnut, Cranberry, and Corn Muffin Bread Pudding

YIELD: 6 to 8 servings

PREPARATION TIME: 25 minutes

COOKING TIME: 3 to 4 hours on HIGH for the bread pudding;
2$\frac{1}{2}$ to 5 hours for the chestnuts

SLOW COOKER SIZE: 4 quart

2 tablespoons butter

1 medium onion, peeled and minced

3 extra-large eggs

1$\frac{1}{2}$ cups milk

$\frac{3}{4}$ cup heavy cream

1$\frac{1}{2}$ tablespoons fresh thyme leaves

$\frac{3}{4}$ teaspoon baking powder

1 teaspoon salt

$\frac{1}{2}$ teaspoon freshly ground black pepper

$\frac{1}{4}$ teaspoon grated nutmeg

2 cups chestnut pieces from Braised Chestnuts (page 12), or coarsely chopped pecans

1$\frac{1}{4}$ cups dried apple rings, quartered

$\frac{2}{3}$ cup dried cranberries

MOVE OVER, STUFFING. HERE IS A BREAD PUD-
ding that easily takes the place of stuffing at Thanksgiving or at any other meal with turkey as the main event. It
pairs up perfectly with ham, pork, or roast beef, and would
be right at home at a breakfast or brunch buffet. Colorful
layers of cranberry, apple, and chestnuts alternate with layers of corn muffin and bread in this savory New England–
style pudding.

Use 1 tablespoon of the butter to generously coat the interior surfaces of the insert of the slow cooker.

Melt the remaining 1 tablespoon butter in a medium sauté pan
over medium heat. Add the onions and cook very slowly, stirring
frequently, until the onion is translucent. Set aside to cool slightly.

In a large bowl combine the eggs, milk, cream, thyme, baking
powder, salt, pepper, and nutmeg. Whisk well, and add the cooked
onions. In a medium bowl combine the chestnuts or pecans, apple
pieces, and cranberries. Toss them together to mix well. Set aside.

In another medium bowl combine the muffin crumbs with the
bread cubes. Place one third of the corn and bread crumbs in the
bottom of the insert. Sprinkle with one third of the chestnut mix-

3 cups coarsely crumbled corn muffin crumbs (about two large 6-ounce corn muffins)

3 cups day-old French bread cubes (¾-inch cubes)

ture. Ladle one third of the egg mixture over the crumbs. Repeat this layering twice more. Cover and cook on HIGH for at least 3 hours, until the top is light golden brown and an instant-read thermometer inserted into the center registers 190°F. Serve hot or warm.

Risotto with Parmesan

YIELD: 4 servings

COOKING TIME: 2 hours on HIGH

SLOW COOKER SIZE: 4 to 6 quart

¼ cup olive oil

2 shallots, peeled and minced

1¼ cups raw arborio rice

¼ cup dry white wine

3¾ cups low-sodium chicken broth, or Chicken Stock (page 8)

1 teaspoon salt

½ to ⅔ cup freshly grated Parmesan cheese, preferably Parmigiano-Reggiano

BELIEVE IT OR NOT, YOU CAN ALSO MAKE RISOTTO in the slow cooker and not spend a minute stirring or watching over it. Relax with a glass of wine and let the machine do the work.

Heat the oil in a small sauté pan over medium heat and sauté the shallots until they have softened. Scrape them into the insert of the slow cooker. (If your microwave oven is large enough to hold the slow cooker insert, place the oil and shallots in the insert of the slow cooker, cover with the inverted lid or a flat plate, place the insert in the microwave, and cook on HIGH for 4 to 5 minutes, or until the shallots have softened.)

Toss the rice in the insert to coat it with the oil. Stir in the wine, broth, and salt. Cover and cook on HIGH for about 2 hours, or until all the liquid is absorbed. Just before serving, stir in the cheese.

VARIATIONS: Add 1 teaspoon of the dried herb of your choice along with the rice.

For a risotto that's out of this world, substitute the juices from Caramelized Onions (page 10) for some of the chicken broth, and then add 1 cup of the Caramelized Onions at the end of the cooking time.

Add ½ cup Duxelles (page 11) to the insert at the start of the cooking time. When the risotto is done, drizzle a bit of white truffle oil on each serving.

To make a risotto like the one traditionally served with Osso Buco (page 101), steep ¼ teaspoon crushed saffron threads in ¼ cup boiling chicken broth or water. Add this mixture to the insert when you add the other cooking liquid and proceed with the recipe.

Wild Rice

YIELD: 6 to 8 servings; 4 cups

COOKING TIME: 2 to 2½ hours on HIGH

SLOW COOKER SIZE: 4 to 6 quart

1 cup raw wild rice

3 cups low-sodium chicken or beef broth, vegetable broth, Chicken Stock (page 8), Vegetable Stock (page 9), or water

1 teaspoon salt

½ teaspoon freshly ground black pepper

2 tablespoons butter

THE NUTTY TASTE OF WILD RICE, MADE EASY IN the slow cooker, is a perfect complement to game, meat, and poultry.

Place the rice in a strainer and rinse it well under running water to remove any dirt particles. Place the rice, broth, salt, pepper, and butter in the insert of the slow cooker and cook on HIGH for 2 to 3 hours, until the rice is slightly crunchy and about half the kernels have opened to expose a white interior. Drain off any excess liquid before serving.

Annatto Rice

YIELD: about 5 cups; 4 servings

COOKING TIME: 2½ hours on LOW

SLOW COOKER SIZE: 4 quart

3 tablespoons annatto oil
(see Note)

Half a medium onion, chopped

1 small carrot, peeled and cut
into ¼-inch dice

1 celery stalk, cut into ¼-inch
dice

2 garlic cloves, peeled and
minced

4 ounces assorted wild
mushrooms, cleaned and thinly
sliced (1½ cups)

Fresh corn kernels cut from 1
small ear (½ cup)

1 teaspoon ground cinnamon

1 cup raw long-grain white rice

2 cups low-sodium chicken broth
or Chicken Stock (page 8)

¾ teaspoon salt

¼ teaspoon freshly ground black
pepper

½ cup goat cheese, crumbled

½ cup chopped fresh cilantro

THIS DISH IS ADAPTED FROM A RECIPE IN RESTAU-rateur Stephan Pyles's innovative book *The New Texas Cuisine*. Here rice and vegetables are seasoned and colored by annatto oil, which is made by steeping bright orange annatto (or achiote) seeds in warmed vegetable oil. You may be able to find annatto oil with other Hispanic foods in your supermarket. If not, the seeds are readily available, and making your own oil takes little work (see Note). Be sure to choose seeds that are bright orange in color; brown ones are old and lack flavor.

Heat the annatto oil in a large sauté pan over medium-high heat. Add the onion, carrot, and celery and cook, stirring until softened, about 3 minutes. Add the garlic, mushrooms, and corn and continue to cook for 3 minutes more. Add the cinnamon and rice and cook for 1 minute to coat the rice grains with oil.

Scrape the mixture into the insert of the slow cooker. Pour the broth into the sauté pan and bring to a boil, scraping down the sides to deglaze the pan. Add the salt and pepper, and then pour the broth over the rice mixture. Stir, cover, and cook on LOW for 2½ hours, until the liquid is absorbed and the rice is tender. Just before serving, swirl in the goat cheese. Sprinkle each serving with some chopped cilantro.

NOTE: To make your own annatto oil, place 1 cup of vegetable oil in a small saucepan with ¼ cup of annatto seeds. Heat the oil until it just starts to bubble and remove the pan from the heat. Let the oil steep for 4 hours, and then strain the oil into a clean jar. The oil will keep in the refrigerator for at least 6 months.

Desserts

Flourless Pear Anise Soufflé

Yield: 4 to 5 servings

Cooking time: 12 to 15 minutes for the soufflé; 4 to 6 hours for the purée

Slow cooker size: 3 quart

3 cups Pear Anise Purée
(page 18)

1 tablespoon unsalted butter,
softened

1 tablespoon granulated sugar

5 extra-large egg whites, at room
temperature

½ cup superfine sugar

1 tablespoon confectioners'
sugar

I USED TO WORK IN A FRENCH RESTAURANT ON Cape Cod. One of my jobs was to make soufflés using an intense fruit purée. I'm sure everyone thought that there was some genius performing magic in the kitchen when the waiter whisked out the quivering airy confection. In fact, it was just me and a recipe for making practically no-fail souffles. This recipe, which can be prepared ahead and baked just before serving, offers great taste, heavenly texture, and a dramatic presentation.

Place the pear purée in a sauté pan over medium heat and bring it to a simmer. Cook the purée, stirring occasionally, until it has reduced by one third and is quite thick. Remove the pan from the heat and transfer the purée to a medium metal bowl to cool completely. This purée is called the "base" of the soufflé.

While the purée is cooling, generously coat the inside of the insert of the slow cooker with the butter, and then dust with the granulated sugar. Put in the freezer. Preheat an oven to 425°F with a rack in the lowest position. Place a heavy-duty baking sheet on the rack.

Put the egg whites in the bowl of an electric mixer. (Make sure that the bowl and beaters are scrupulously clean.) Beat on a high speed until they begin to get foamy and opaque. Continue to beat while you gradually add the superfine sugar. Beat until the whites form substantial, soft peaks; overbeating them causes the whites to become dry. Take a generous spoonful of whites and stir them into the cooled pear purée to lighten it. Now add the purée to the beaten egg whites and use a rubber spatula to fold the purée into the whites, forming a homogeneous mixture.

Remove the prepared insert from the freezer. Pour and scrape the fruit mixture into the insert, mounding it higher in the center than on the sides. Place in the oven on the baking sheet, and immediately lower the oven temperature to 400°F. Bake until the soufflé has risen up to or over the rim of the insert and the top is a deep, golden brown, 12 to 15 minutes. Remove the soufflé from the oven, sprinkle with the confectioners' sugar, and serve immediately. Use two large serving spoons to scoop the soufflé from the center.

Pear Sorbet

YIELD: 6 servings; 1 quart

COOKING TIME: 4 to 6 hours for the purée

1 recipe Pear Anise Purée
(page 18), chilled

THIS AMAZING RECIPE GIVES NO-FAT DESSERTS a positive spin. The anise is barely discernable, yet lends a slight smokiness to the pear's sweetness. It was a huge hit after a big Thanksgiving dinner—some folks even passed on the pumpkin pie and went straight for the sorbet, and then had seconds!

Place the purée in an ice-cream machine and freeze according to the manufacturer's instructions.

Deux Pears
Poached in Champagne

YIELD: 4 servings

COOKING TIME: 3 to 4 hours on HIGH

SLOW COOKER SIZE: 1½ to 2 quart

4 underripe, unblemished whole Comice or Anjou pears, with stems attached

8 whole dried pears, halved lengthwise

Finely grated zest and strained juice of 1 large lemon

3 cups Champagne, plus more if needed

1 cup granulated sugar

L ARGE COMICE PEARS ARE FLAVORFUL ENOUGH to stand up to the Champagne in this refreshing, yet satisfying dessert. This makes a beautiful presentation—the white pears, stems still in place, and the golden accent of the dried pears. The slow cooker must be deep enough to accommodate the pears sitting upright (it's fine if they touch each other). Any kind of Champagne (dry, semidry, sweet, or rosé) will do fine for this recipe. You can even use leftover Champagne that's gone flat.

Working from the bottom of each pear, use a sharp paring knife or grapefruit spoon to dig out the core and seeds. Peel the pears, leaving the stems in place. Set aside. Use the dried pear halves to line the bottom of the insert of the slow cooker. Place the whole pears, standing upright, on top. In a medium bowl stir together the lemon zest and juice, Champagne, and sugar. Pour this mixture over the pears, making sure the liquid comes at least halfway up the sides of the pears. Pour in more Champagne if necessary.

Cover and cook on HIGH for 3 to 4 hours, or until the fresh and dried pears are tender when pierced with the tip of a sharp knife. Turn off the slow cooker and allow the pears to cool in the syrup. To serve, place a pear in each of 4 rimmed plates or shallow bowls. Add 1 or 2 pieces of dried pear, and spoon on some syrup.

Triple Applesauce Granita

YIELD: 4 to 6 servings

COOKING TIME: 3 to 6 hours for the applesauce

4 cups Triple Applesauce (page 19), well chilled

¼ cup Calvados or apple brandy, optional

THE TRIPLE APPLESAUCE (PAGE 19) MAKES A fabulous frozen dessert base. You can use an ice-cream maker, or simply freeze it in a shallow metal pan according to the directions below. The ice-cream maker will yield a product with the smooth texture of a sorbet; using a pan in the freezer will produce a granular texture with larger ice crystals.

If you are using an ice-cream maker, place the applesauce in the container and freeze according to the manufacturer's instructions. Otherwise, place a shallow metal pan with at least a 5-cup capacity in the freezer 1 hour before you plan to make the granita. Place the applesauce in the chilled pan, cover it with aluminum foil, and return it to the freezer. Stir the mixture every 20 to 30 minutes with a fork, returning the covered pan to the freezer each time, until the granita is "soft" (frozen slightly slushy), with coarse crystals of ice. This will probably take 2 to 4 hours.

To serve the frozen granita, spoon it into small cups and add a splash of Calvados, if desired, to each serving.

The World's Best Vanilla Ice Cream

YIELD: about 3½ cups

COOKING TIME: 4 hours on LOW or 2 hours on HIGH

SLOW COOKER SIZE: 1 quart

1 cup granulated sugar

2 cups heavy cream

1 large vanilla bean, split lengthwise

1 cup mascarpone cheese, or regular cream cheese (not whipped)

HAVE YOU EVER TASTED VANILLA ICE CREAM made with a real vanilla bean? If not, you're in for a shock! That poor imitation you've been burying under a blanket of chocolate sauce and whipped cream needs all the help it can get, while the "right stuff" needs nothing more than a spoon to seduce your taste buds. Making the base in the slow cooker slowly infuses the cream and sugar with vanilla essence. When it's done, you can rinse the vanilla bean and reuse it in another recipe. I've replaced the traditional egg yolks with mascarpone, a soft Italian cheese found in the dairy or cheese section of many supermarkets, which lends creamy smoothness to the ice cream.

Place the sugar, heavy cream, and vanilla bean in the insert of the slow cooker. Cover and cook on LOW for 4 hours or on HIGH for 2 hours. Turn off the slow cooker and let the cream mixture cool, covered, for 15 minutes. Whisk in the mascarpone or cream cheese. Stir until very smooth. Chill completely, and then freeze in an ice-cream maker according to the manufacturer's directions.

Chestnut Ice Cream

YIELD: 6 servings; 1 quart

COOKING TIME: 2½ to 5 hours for the braised chestnuts; 8 to 12 hours for candying the chestnuts

1½ cups Candied Chestnuts in Syrup (page 20)

2 teaspoons pure vanilla extract

4 cups heavy cream

2 extra-large eggs, lightly beaten

Bittersweet Chocolate Sauce (recipe follows)

THERE IS A VERY SPECIAL ICE-CREAM SHOP ON the Île St-Louis in Paris called Berthillon, where they make ice cream in dozens of heavenly flavors. My favorite flavor is *marron*, made with chestnut purée, heavy cream, and rum. Served alone, it's fabulous. Topped with some Bittersweet Chocolate Sauce, it's perfection.

Place the candied chestnuts and vanilla in the bowl of a food processor fitted with a metal blade or in a blender. Process or blend just to combine, 15 to 20 seconds. Leave the mixture in the processor bowl or blender. Position a fine mesh sieve over a 2-quart metal bowl.

Place the heavy cream and eggs in a medium saucepan over medium-high heat. Heat the mixture, stirring constantly with a wooden spoon, until it just starts to thicken and lightly coats the spoon. Don't let the mixture boil or the eggs will curdle. Remove the saucepan from the heat and immediately pour the mixture through the sieve and allow it to cool in the metal bowl for 5 minutes. With the processor or blender running, slowly pour the cooled cream and egg mixture into the puréed chestnuts. Process or blend until smooth, scraping down the sides of the container once or twice.

Pour the chestnut and cream mixture into a clean metal bowl, cover, and refrigerate until cold, at least 4 hours or overnight. Freeze in an ice-cream machine according to the manufacturer's directions. Serve with Bittersweet Chocolate Sauce.

Bittersweet Chocolate Sauce

YIELD: 3$\frac{1}{2}$ cups

COOKING TIME: about 25 minutes

2 cups heavy cream

$\frac{1}{2}$ cup packed dark brown sugar

8 ounces bittersweet chocolate, chopped

2 ounces unsweetened chocolate, chopped

3 tablespoons unsalted butter, cut into small pieces

2 to 3 tablespoons rum, preferably dark, optional

Place the cream in a large saucepan over medium-high heat and bring to a boil, but do not let it overflow the sides of the pan. Reduce the heat to a simmer and cook until the cream has reduced by half, 15 to 20 minutes. Stir in the brown sugar and heat, stirring, until dissolved. Remove from the heat and stir in the bittersweet and unsweetened chocolate and the butter. Stir until the chocolate and butter have melted and the mixture is smooth. Add the rum, if desired.

Dulce de Leche
Whipped Cream or Ice Cream

YIELD: about 3 cups of whipped cream, and 2½ cups of ice cream

2 cups heavy cream

½ cup Dulce de Leche
(page 21)

You haven't lived until you've spooned some softly whipped heavy cream flavored with Dulce de Leche (page 21) on top of hot coffee (fortified with rum, if you are looking for the ultimate sweet treat), or turned that flavored cream into ice cream.

Scald the heavy cream in a small saucepan over medium-high heat, until tiny bubbles appear around the rim of the pan. Remove from the heat and whisk in the dulce de leche until it dissolves and the mixture is smooth. Pour into a deep metal bowl and refrigerate until it is very cold. Beat the mixture with a whisk or electric mixer until it forms soft peaks. Spoon on top of hot coffee, milk shakes, ice cream, or cake.

To make Dulce de Leche Ice Cream, remove the dulce de leche–flavored cream from the refrigerator and spoon into an ice-cream maker. Freeze according to the manufacturer's directions.

Prunes in Armagnac

YIELD: about 4 cups

COOKING TIME: 8 hours on LOW or 6 hours on HIGH

SLOW COOKER SIZE: 3 quart

1 pound jumbo pitted prunes

Finely grated zest of 1 large lemon

1 cup Armagnac

1½ cups freshly squeezed and strained orange juice

THIS IS A CLASSIC FRENCH RECIPE THAT CAN BE used as a garnish for fowl or game dishes. My very favorite application, however, is to use these prunes to make what has to be the world's most sensuous, seductive, non-chocolate dessert, Prunes in a Pitcher (page 176). Armagnac, like cognac, gets its color and flavor from being aged in oak. I love to eat this as is on top of hot oatmeal, or spoon some on top of a broiled grapefruit half.

Place the prunes, lemon zest, Armagnac, and orange juice in the insert of the slow cooker. Cover and cook on LOW for 8 hours or on HIGH for 6 hours, until most of the liquid is absorbed and the prunes are very soft.

Store in the refrigerator in a tightly sealed container for up to 3 months.

Prunes in a Pitcher

YIELD: 6 servings

COOKING TIME: 6 to 8 hours for the prunes

1 quart heavy cream (not ultra-pasteurized, if possible)

1 recipe Prunes in Armagnac (page 175)

THIS RECIPE APPEARED IN THE *NEW YORK TIMES* years ago. I'm not sure where the pitcher tradition came from, but I use a rustic white pottery pitcher and a small ladle.

Pour the cream into a large saucepan set over medium heat. Bring to a simmer, and then lower the heat and continue to simmer until the cream has reduced by one third. Chill thoroughly.

To serve, put the prunes and any cooking liquid in a large, attractive pitcher. Pour the reduced cream over the top. Ladle the prunes and cream into small bowls.

Mont Blanc

YIELD: 6 servings

COOKING TIME: $2\frac{1}{2}$ to 5 hours for the braised chestnuts; 8 to 12 hours for candying the chestnuts

2 cups heavy cream, well chilled

10 ounces bittersweet chocolate, chopped

2 tablespoons unsalted butter

1 recipe Candied Chestnuts in Syrup (page 12), puréed (see the variation in that recipe) and chilled

A FAIRYLAND CONCOCTION OF SWEETENED CHEST-nut purée, chocolate sauce, and whipped cream, this grown-up dessert calls for Mozart in the background, candlelight, and perhaps a little Champagne to wash it down.

Beat 1 cup of the heavy cream with a whisk or electric mixer until it forms soft peaks. Set aside.

Heat the remaining 1 cup of heavy cream in a medium saucepan over medium heat. When tiny bubbles appear around the edge of the pan, remove it from the heat and stir in the chocolate. When it has melted and the mixture is smooth, stir in the butter. Cool the mixture to room temperature.

To assemble the desserts, spoon ⅓ cup of the puréed candied chestnuts into a small, wide-mesh sieve. Hold the sieve over a small dessert dish or shallow bowl.

Use a wooden spoon to push the purée through the sieve into the center of the dish to form a miniature mountain. Repeat the process on 5 more plates. Drizzle chocolate sauce over the top of each serving and garnish with a generous dollop of whipped cream. Serve immediately.

Chocolate Chestnut Soufflé

YIELD: 4 to 5 servings

COOKING TIME: 25 to 30 minutes for the soufflé; 2½ to 5 hours for the braised chestnuts; 8 to 12 hours for candying the chestnuts

2 tablespoons unsalted butter

1 cup plus 1 tablespoon granulated sugar

½ cup whole milk

1 tablespoon instant or quick-mixing flour, such as Wondra™

4 ounces bittersweet chocolate, chopped

4 ounces unsweetened chocolate, chopped

4 extra-large eggs, separated, at room temperature

½ cup chestnuts from Candied Chestnuts in Syrup (page 20), crumbled

½ cup syrup from Candied Chestnuts in Syrup

¼ cup rum

MAKING A HOT SOUFFLÉ USED TO MEAN STOP-ping everything while you whipped it up at the last minute, and then holding up dinner while it cooked. You can make this soufflé up to 4 hours ahead to the point where it is about to be baked, and place it in the refrigerator. Pop it in the oven in the middle of the main course.

This is not a high-rising soufflé, but it might rise 1 inch beyond the top of the soufflé dish. If you are planning to bake the soufflé immediately, preheat the oven to 400°F with the rack positioned so that the risen soufflé will not hit the top of the oven. If you are not baking the soufflé now, make room in the coldest part of your refrigerator for the soufflé dish.

Soften 1 tablespoon of the butter and generously coat the interior of an 8-inch soufflé dish that is 2½ inches high with a 6-cup capacity. Sprinkle the interior with 1 tablespoon of the sugar and set aside.

In a medium saucepan set over medium heat combine ¾ cup of the sugar with the milk. Bring the mixture to a rolling boil and whisk in the flour. Cook for 1 minute more. Remove the saucepan from the heat and stir in the bittersweet and unsweetened chocolate, and then whisk gently until the mixture is smooth. Whisk in the remaining 1 tablespoon of butter, and then whisk in the egg yolks, one at a time, until completely blended.

In a clean bowl, using an electric mixer with clean beaters, beat the egg whites with the remaining ¼ cup sugar until stiff, but not dry. Stir a large spoonful of whites into the chocolate mixture to lighten it and then fold the chocolate mixture into the whites with a large rubber spatula, trying not to deflate the whites, until there are just a few streaks of white remaining. Spoon half the mixture into the prepared soufflé dish. Sprinkle with the chestnuts. Add the remaining egg and chocolate mixture. (At this point the soufflé can be baked, or it can be covered with plastic wrap and refrigerated for up to 4 hours.)

Bake the soufflé for 20 minutes at 400°F, and then reduce the oven temperature to 350°F and bake for an additional 5 to 10 minutes. The soufflé will not rise dramatically, but the top should be very crusty and the soufflé should be firm and not wiggle much when the dish is shaken.

While the soufflé is baking, combine the chestnut syrup and rum in a small saucepan and cook over low heat until it barely simmers. Continue cooking for 1 minute and remove from the heat.

Remove the soufflé from the oven. Use two large spoons to gently make a opening in the center. Pour in the warm syrup, and serve immediately.

Hazelnut Chocolate Fondue

YIELD: 6 servings

COOKING TIME: 45 to 60 minutes on HIGH

SLOW COOKER SIZE: 1 quart

10 ounces hazelnut milk chocolate (gianduja), chopped

1 cup heavy cream

A selection of fresh fruit (strawberries, bananas, oranges or star fruit), cut into chunks, or hard cookies (such as biscotti and shortbread), or pretzels, for dipping

GIANDUJA IS MILK CHOCOLATE THAT HAS BEEN mixed with hazelnut paste. Thanks to specialty food importers, this Italian ingredient is now easy to find in catalogues such as the King Arthur Baker's Catalogue (800-827-6836; www.kingarthurflour.com), and in gourmet food stores. Fondue made from gianduja combines the best of all worlds: the silky smoothness of milk chocolate, the mellow richness of toasted hazelnuts, and the spark of strawberries, raspberries, peaches, and any other fruit you care to dip. This is a grown-up dessert, but I'll bet the kids will want a taste.

Place the chocolate pieces in the insert of the slow cooker. Pour in the cream. Set the slow cooker on HIGH and cook, *uncovered*, for about 45 minutes, stirring occasionally, until the chocolate is completely melted and well blended with the cream. As soon as it is thoroughly smooth, it is ready to serve.

Use fondue forks, long wooden skewers, or even table forks to spear fruit or cookies. Dip them in the chocolate to coat, and then eat.

Marbled Cheesecake
with Dulce de Leche

YIELD: 12 servings

COOKING TIME: 1¼ hours, plus 1 hour in a turned-off oven for the cheesecake;
10 hours for the dulce de leche

FOR THE CRUST

1 tablespoon softened butter

2 cups finely ground graham
cracker crumbs

⅓ cup pecans, finely chopped

¼ cup packed light brown sugar

½ teaspoon ground cinnamon

6 tablespoons unsalted butter,
melted

FOR THE FILLING

3 (8-ounce) packages
Philadelphia Brand cream
cheese, at room temperature
(not whipped, reduced-fat,
or no-fat)

½ cup granulated sugar

2 tablespoons cornstarch

4 extra-large eggs

1 tablespoon pure vanilla extract

1 cup Dulce de Leche (page 21)

THIS RECIPE IS ADAPTED FROM ONE OFFERED BY Victoria Riccardi in her article in the *Boston Globe*. Hang onto your hats and invite your twelve best friends over for dessert. By making the cheesecake filling in the food processor, you avoid getting bubbles in the batter, which lessens the chances that the top will crack during baking.

Preheat the oven to 350°F with a rack at the center position. Wrap the outside of a 10-inch springform pan, bottom and sides, with a double layer of aluminum foil. Coat the inside of the pan generously with the 1 tablespoon softened butter. To make the crust, in a medium mixing bowl toss together the crumbs, nuts, brown sugar, and cinnamon. Stir in the melted butter. Press the crumb mixture gently into the bottom and halfway up the sides of the buttered pan.

Place the cream cheese and sugar in the bowl of a food processor fitted with the metal blade. Sift the cornstarch over the mixture, and process until smooth. Add the eggs and vanilla and continue to process until smooth, scraping down the sides of the bowl as necessary.

Scoop 1 cup of the filling into a small mixing bowl, and stir in the dulce de leche. Stir to combine the mixture well, and set aside. Bring a kettle of water to a boil.

Scrape the filling from the food processor into the prepared springform pan, and smooth the top with a rubber spatula. Spoon dollops of the dulce-de-leche mixture onto the plain batter, leaving 1 to 2 inches between dollops. Hold a butter knife perpendicular to the pan and gently cut through the filling to swirl the darker dulce-de-leche filling into the lighter one. Don't overdo it, or you will lose the marbled effect.

Place the springform pan in a large roasting pan and pour enough of the boiling water into the roasting pan to come 1½ inches up the side of the cheesecake pan. Bake the cheesecake for 1 to 1¼ hours, until the center is set and no longer jiggles when the pan is gently moved. Turn off the oven, leave the oven door slightly ajar, and let the cheesecake sit for 1 more hour.

Remove the cheesecake from the water bath and remove the aluminum foil. Place the springform pan on a wire rack and allow the cake to cool completely in the pan, then cover the top securely with aluminum foil. Refrigerate for 6 hours or overnight, until the cake is very cold. Just before serving, run a sharp knife around the inside edge of the pan and remove the sides. Use a knife rinsed in hot water to cut the cake into thin wedges.

Pumpkin Bread Pudding with
Bourbon Caramel Sauce and Whipped Cream

YIELD: 6 to 8 servings; 2 cups of sauce

COOKING TIME: 3½ hours on LOW for the pudding; 15 to 20 minutes on the stove top for the sauce

SLOW COOKER SIZE: 4 quart

FOR THE BREAD PUDDING

1 (1-pound) loaf challah or firm-textured French bread, cut into 1½-inch cubes (4½ cups)

1½ tablespoons unsalted butter, softened

1½ cups heavy cream

1½ cups whole milk

1 cup canned unseasoned pumpkin purée

1½ teaspoons ground cinnamon

Heaping ¼ teaspoon ground nutmeg

⅛ teaspoon ground allspice

2 extra-large eggs

2 extra-large egg yolks

⅓ cup packed light brown sugar

1½ teaspoons pure vanilla extract

¼ teaspoon salt

WHEN EMMY MADE THIS, I JUST ABOUT swooned. She actually had to grab the spoon away from me. We're talking seriously amazingly good dessert here. This is not for someone who is looking for a light end to a meal; it's a real dessert-lover's dream come true. As far as I'm concerned, you can just forget about the rest of the meal. Bring on the Pumpkin Bread Pudding, and don't hold back on the Bourbon Caramel Sauce.

Preheat the oven to 350°F with a rack at the center position. Place the bread cubes on a rimmed baking pan and bake for 10 to 15 minutes to dry them out. Use ½ tablespoon of the butter to coat the inside of the insert of the slow cooker. Press the bread cubes into the bottom; they should fit snugly, and the bottom should be thoroughly covered. Turn the slow cooker to HIGH and let it heat, uncovered, while you prepare the pudding.

In a medium saucepan heat the cream and milk until the mixture is very hot and starts to bubble, but do not let it boil. Remove from the heat. Place the pumpkin purée, cinnamon, nutmeg, allspice, eggs and egg yolks, brown sugar, vanilla, and salt in a large mixing bowl. Whisk them together well, and then slowly pour in the hot cream mixture, whisking constantly.

Turn the slow cooker down to LOW. Carefully pour the pumpkin and cream mixture over the bread and push the bread pieces down beneath the mixture to moisten them. (They will pop up

FOR THE BOURBON CARAMEL SAUCE AND WHIPPED CREAM

2 cups granulated sugar

1 cup water

1 tablespoon strained lemon juice

4 tablespoons unsalted butter, at room temperature, cut into 4 pieces

2½ cups heavy cream, well chilled

⅓ cup bourbon

1 tablespoon pure vanilla extract

again; that's okay.) Dot the top with the remaining 1 tablespoon of softened butter. Cover and cook for 3½ hours on LOW, or until an instant-read thermometer inserted in the center registers 190°F and a small knife inserted in the center comes out clean. Turn the slow cooker off and let the pudding rest, covered, for 30 minutes.

While the pudding is cooking, make the Bourbon Caramel Sauce. Have all the ingredients ready before you begin. Place the sugar, water, and lemon juice in a large heavy saucepan. (It must have at least a 2-quart capacity because the mixture will bubble vigorously when the cream and butter are added later, and you don't want to get burned.) Bring the sugar mixture to a boil over medium-high heat; stir only until the sugar is dissolved and the syrup is clear. Continue to boil, without stirring, until the mixture starts to turn an amber color, which may take as long as 15 to 20 minutes. (Be careful, because it can burn very easily; if your eyes begin to sting it means it is starting to burn.) When the mixture has darkened to a rich caramel color, remove it from the heat and immediately stir in the butter, bit by bit, then ½ cup of the heavy cream, and finally the bourbon and vanilla. Cool to room temperature.

While the sauce is cooling, beat the remaining 2 cups of cream with a whisk or electric mixer until it forms soft peaks.

To serve the pudding, scoop it into individual bowls, drizzle on some caramel sauce, then top with a dollop of whipped cream.

Rum-Croissant Bread Pudding
with Fantasy Cherry Sauce

YIELD: 6 to 8 servings

COOKING TIME: 1 hour on HIGH, and then 3 hours on LOW (4 hours total)

SLOW COOKER SIZE: 4 quart

2 tablespoons unsalted butter, softened

2 cups whole milk

2 cups heavy cream

4 extra-large eggs

½ cup packed dark brown sugar

⅓ cup rum

1½ teaspoons pure vanilla extract

½ cup pecan halves

5 large plain stale croissants, cut lengthwise into thirds

Fantasy Cherry Sauce (recipe follows)

IF YOU ARE LOOKING FOR AN INDULGENT DISH TO serve a crowd, you've come to the right place. This bread pudding will not only make a gorgeous centerpiece; it will also satisfy the sweet tooth of every dessert-lover you know. Leaving the croissants out, uncovered, overnight will get them stale enough for this recipe. Since different slow cookers cook at different temperatures, the best way to judge when this is done is to use an instant-read thermometer. You'll need a large slow cooker.

Use the softened butter to generously coat the inside of the insert of the slow cooker.

In a large bowl combine the milk, cream, eggs, dark brown sugar, rum, vanilla, and pecans. Stir well to mix.

Divide the croissant pieces into four portions. Overlap one portion in the bottom of the insert. Pour in one-third of the milk mixture. Add another overlapping layer of croissant pieces, then pour in one-half of the remaining milk mixture. Make a third layer of croissants, and then pour in the remaining milk mixture. Layer the last portion of croissants on top.

Cover the slow cooker and cook on HIGH for 1 hour, and then reduce the heat to LOW and cook until the custard is set and an instant-read thermometer inserted into the center of the pudding registers 190°F, about 3 hours. Serve hot or at room temperature, with Fantasy Cherry Sauce.

Fantasy Cherry Sauce

YIELD: about 2 cups

COOKING TIME: 10 minutes

2 cups packed dried pitted Bing or other sweet cherries

3 cups orange juice

⅓ cup kirsch

Place the cherries, orange juice, and kirsch in a large saucepan. Bring to a boil over medium-high heat and simmer, uncovered, for 10 minutes. Let the sauce cool in the pan. Serve hot, warm, or at room temperature. Store in a tightly covered container in the refrigerator for up to 6 months.

Indian Pudding

YIELD: 6 to 8 servings

COOKING TIME: 9 hours on LOW

SLOW COOKER SIZE: 4 quart

½ yellow cornmeal

4 cups whole milk

¼ cup regular (not blackstrap) molasses

2 tablespoons granulated sugar

¼ teaspoon salt

Pinch of baking soda

2 tablespoons butter, cut into 4 pieces

1 extra-large egg, lightly beaten

BESIDES OUR FRIENDSHIP, EMMY AND I SHARE A passion for an ever-lengthening list of things. A few examples are Lucinda Williams, certain women writers, pets that are as important as people, Lily Tomlin, more cookbooks than you could ever read, and Indian pudding. In our search for a heart-stopping, 10-on-the-Richter-scale version of this dish, we've had more losers than winners; more soggy, leaden disappointments, in which the vanilla ice cream melting on top was the best part of the dish. When Emmy announced that she thought she could make a great Indian pudding in the slow cooker, I was, to say the least, skeptical; but, hey, why discourage her? Thank God I didn't! I'm thrilled to announce, ladies and gentlemen, that it can be done, and superbly! With great reverence I present you with Emmy's triple-A Indian Pudding.

Place the cornmeal in a medium heavy-bottomed saucepan. Pour in 2 cups of the milk; whisk constantly as you pour, so that the cornmeal does not form lumps. Whisk in the molasses, sugar, salt, baking soda, butter, and egg. Set the saucepan over medium-high heat and cook the mixture, whisking constantly and making sure to reach into the corners of the pan, until small bubbles start to form on the surface and the mixture starts to thicken. Remove from the heat and immediately add the remaining 2 cups of milk, whisking vigorously to dissolve any lumps.

Pour the mixture into the insert of the slow cooker. Cover and cook on LOW for 9 hours, or until the outer edges and top have darkened and the middle is almost set. Turn off the slow cooker and let the pudding cool slightly, uncovered. Serve with The World's Best Vanilla Ice Cream (page 171) or a store-bought variety.

Coconut Rice Pudding

YIELD: 6 cups

COOKING TIME: 5 hours on LOW or 3 hours on HIGH

SLOW COOKER SIZE: 4 quart

1 cup raw white arborio rice

4 cups half-and-half

1 (14-ounce) can coconut milk

⅔ cup granulated sugar

THIS RICE PUDDING, WITH ITS DELICATE coconut flavor, is luscious comfort food. Served warm, it fills you with a heavenly sense of sweet contentment. To dress it up, sprinkle with toasted shredded coconut, or for an even classier presentation, serve with puréed mango, seasoned with lime juice and/or sugar.

Place the rice in the insert of the slow cooker.

Stir together half-and-half, coconut milk, and sugar in a large, heavy saucepan. Place over medium-high heat and cook, stirring, until the mixture is very warm and the sugar has dissolved. Pour the mixture over the rice, stir well, and then cover and cook on LOW for 5 hours OR on HIGH for 3 hours. The pudding will bubble and the rice will be very soft. Turn the cooker off and let the pudding sit for 30 minutes before serving.

Rice Pudding
with Raisins

YIELD: 6 cups

COOKING TIME: 5 hours on LOW

SLOW COOKER SIZE: 4 quart

1 cup raw white arborio rice

6 cups whole milk

1 (14-ounce) can sweetened condensed milk

1 teaspoon pure vanilla extract

½ teaspoon ground cinnamon

¼ teaspoon salt

½ cup raisins

THERE'S SOMETHING TO BE SAID FOR TRADITION, especially when it comes in the form of classic, creamy, and comforting rice pudding.

Place the rice in the insert of the slow cooker.

Combine the whole milk, sweetened condensed milk, vanilla, cinnamon, and salt in a medium saucepan. Stir together to mix well, and then set the pan over medium-high heat. Heat the mixture until it almost simmers, stirring frequently and making sure to reach into the corners of the saucepan, about 10 minutes. Pour the mixture over the rice, stir well, and cook, covered, on LOW for 3 hours. Quickly uncover the cooker and stir in the raisins. Continue to cook the pudding, covered, for 2 more hours.

Turn off the slow cooker and let the pudding sit, covered, for 30 minutes. The finished pudding will be creamy and soft, with no "bite" left to the rice.

Pear Crumble

YIELD: 6 servings

COOKING TIME: 4 hours on HIGH

SLOW COOKER SIZE: 4 quart

4 Bosc pears, rinsed, cored, and cut into 1-inch cubes

1 packed cup dried pears, coarsely chopped

¾ cup golden raisins

1½ cups packed dark brown sugar

½ cup honey

¾ cup all-purpose flour

¾ cup rolled oats, old-fashioned or quick-cooking (not instant)

8 tablespoons (1 stick) chilled butter, cut into small pieces

1 pint best-quality store-bought vanilla ice cream, or The World's Best Vanilla Ice Cream (page 171)

FRESH AND DRIED PEARS ADD FLAVOR AND sweetness to this homey dessert. After the filling is made in the slow cooker, the topping is added and the dessert is finished in the oven.

Place the fresh and dried pears, raisins, ½ cup of the brown sugar, and the honey in the insert of the slow cooker. Stir well, cover, and cook on HIGH for 3½ hours, or until the fruit is soft. Turn off the slow cooker and carefully remove the insert from the base. Place a mesh strainer or colander over a sauté pan and pour in the contents of the insert. Return the fruit to the insert, leaving the juice in the sauté pan.

Bring the cooking juice to a boil over high heat. Cook, stirring, until the juice becomes thick and syrupy and begins to caramelize. Remove from the heat.

Preheat the oven to 350°F with a rack at the center position. Put the flour, oats, and remaining 1 cup of brown sugar in a medium mixing bowl. Stir with a fork to combine. Use your fingers to work in the butter until the mixture resembles coarse meal.

Distribute the topping over the pear mixture in the insert. Bake for 30 minutes, until the fruit is bubbling and the topping is golden brown. Serve in bowls topped with a scoop of vanilla ice cream. Drizzle some of the hot reduced cooking juices over the ice cream.

Slow Cooker Candied Orange and Grapefruit Peel

YIELD: 50 to 60 pieces

COOKING TIME: 2 to 3 hours on HIGH

SLOW COOKER SIZE: 2 quart

2 large, brightly colored, thick-skinned navel oranges

1 large thick-skinned grapefruit

6 cups water

7 to 8 cups granulated sugar

USING THE SLOW COOKER TO CANDY CITRUS rind is much simpler than the traditional method. There is no need to monitor the process with a candy thermometer or worry about a precise cooking time. Select thick-skinned grapefruit and navel oranges because they yield the most flavorful and colorful results.

Rinse the fruit in several changes of boiling water to remove wax. Use a sharp serrated knife to remove the rind (both the white pith and colored zest) from the fruit, cutting down to, but not into, the fruit. Cut the rind into strips 2 inches long and ¼ inch wide.

Bring the water to a rapid boil in a medium saucepan set over high heat. Add the rind and cook, uncovered, for 5 minutes. Drain the rind and place it in the insert of the slow cooker. Add 3 cups of the sugar and stir briefly just to coat the rind. Cover and cook on HIGH for 2 to 3 hours, or just until the rind is very tender when pierced with a fork. Turn off the slow cooker, leaving the rind and syrup in it.

Line a baking sheet with parchment or foil. Sprinkle 2 cups of the remaining sugar into a rimmed pan or on another baking sheet. Use tongs to transfer the rind, one piece at a time, from the slow cooker to the sugar. Use the tongs or two forks to roll it around until well coated, and then remove it to dry on the parchment or foil. Repeat with the remaining rind, adding sugar as necessary.

As you become more proficient, you'll be able to do several pieces at once; just make sure you coat all sides and that the pieces do not touch each other when you place them on the second baking sheet. Allow the candied peel to dry, uncovered, for 4 to 5 hours, and then store in a sealed container. It will keep at room temperature for up to 1 month. Don't refrigerate this, as the sugar will soften and the peel will get tacky.

Blueberry Conserve

YIELD: about 6 cups

COOKING TIME: 2 hours on HIGH and 2 hours to cool

SLOW COOKER SIZE: 4 quart

2 quarts fresh blueberries, rinsed and picked over

4 tablespoons quick-cooking tapioca

1 cup granulated sugar

Grated zest and strained juice of 1 lemon

I SPEND THE SUMMER ON CAPE COD, WHERE BLUE-berries grow as abundantly as the poison ivy, so when you pick blueberries you have to be careful of where you step. You can use the tiny wild blueberries or the larger cultivated kind to make this thick, luscious conserve that can be spread on toast, spooned over ice cream or French toast, or just eaten straight out of the jar. It also makes a great pie filling for a baked crumb crust. Take care not to try tasting it right out of the slow cooker because it becomes exceedingly hot during cooking.

Place the berries, tapioca, sugar, and lemon zest and juice in the insert of the slow cooker, and stir together to mix. Cover and cook on HIGH for 30 minutes, and then stir again. Cover and continue to cook for another 1½ hours.

Turn the slow cooker off, leave it covered, and allow the conserve to cool to room temperature. Store in covered sterilized containers in the refrigerator.

Index